THE L.I.F.E.
OF A
SPECIAL AGENT

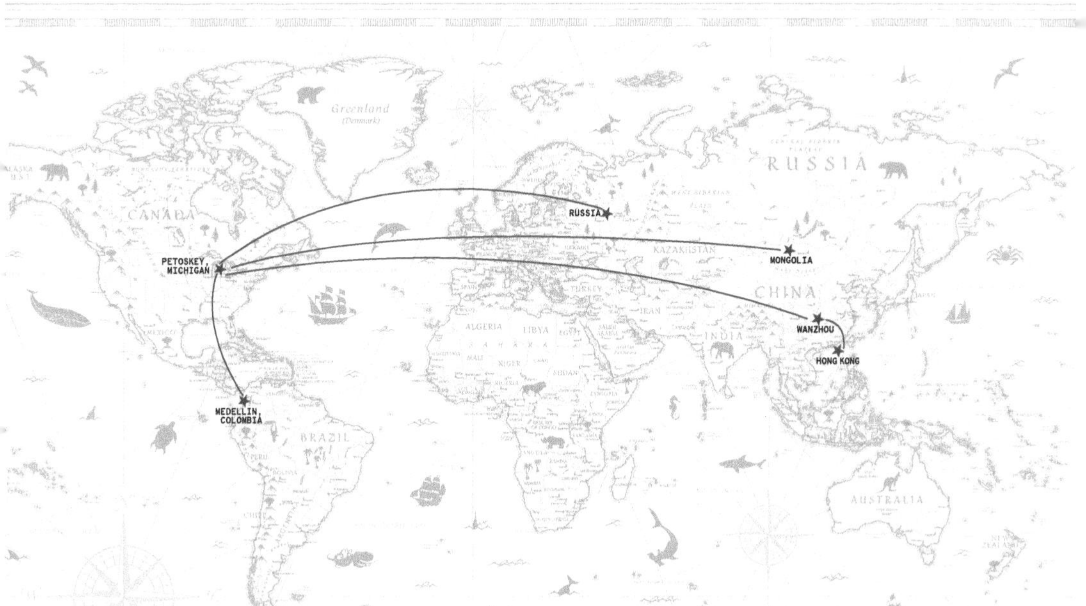

LIFE'S Incredible Adventure Series

IN HIS MAJESTY'S SERVICE

BEN MANTHEI
and
RUTH MANTHEI-WILKEY

In His Majesty's Service

Copyright © 2025 by Ben Manthei and Ruth Manthei-Wilkey

All rights reserved. No part of this publication may be reproduced, distributed, or transmitted in any form or by any means, including photocopying, recording, or other electronic or mechanical methods, without the prior written permission of the author, except in the case of brief quotations embodied in critical reviews and certain other non-commercial uses permitted by copyright law.

Unless otherwise noted, all scripture references are from the King James Bible, public domain.

ISBN: 978-1-7338043-9-4 (Paperback)
   978-1-7338043- (eBook)

Published by Sonflower Press, LLC
3890 Charlevoix Ave. Suite 300
Petoskey, MI 49770

Book design by TeaBerryStudio.com

THANKS

We would like to express our heartfelt thanks to each one who invested their L.I.F.E. into helping us create this book for the glory of God.

Special thanks to Tara Mayberry for an incredible job on the book layout and design. Thanks to Kristine Seelye, Jill Chapman, and Kathy Manthei, whose substantive editorial suggestions raised the quality of our manuscript to a whole new level.

To our extended family, who not only shares our passion but also whose lives inspired and encouraged us on this adventure: Nancy, who shared Ben with the world as he lived out these adventures and worked on the manuscript; Mom, our greatest fan, who fed us while we worked and also edited repeatedly as we progressed; and to our test-readers who offered excellent input and raved enough to keep us going, thank you!

Finally, to our Lord Jesus Christ, who led us into this L.I.F.E. of adventure and allowed us to see His mighty hand at work. What a rush! May He bless your hearts as you read and lead you into an ever-deepening L.I.F.E. of significance and fulfillment.

FOREWORD

Seldom will someone meet not only an individual, but an entire family, that touches their life and sets a new standard of commitment to excellence. For me, the Manthei family has set this standard. Their story began when two brothers married two sisters. Ted and Mary had six boys. The authors are the youngest children of Ernie and Cora, who raised five boys and two girls.

What touched my heart about these families was that both couples raised their children to be hard workers who are committed to excellence, who do it all for the glory of God, and who invest their God-given success into the mission field, principally internationally. We cannot take anything with us when we die, but we can send it ahead by investing in presenting the gospel to others whose lives can be changed for eternity.

The stories reflected here are accounts from the spiritual journeys of Ben Manthei and his extended family and are a reflection of how God uses ordinary people to do extraordinary things. The Manthei family knows that their successes come only from their extraordinary God.

Ben Manthei, and the entire Manthei families of Ted and Ernie, were raised to be involved in mission work. They have labored hard on the job, and they have labored hard on the mission field. This call to service can happen to any of us if we just let God use the gifts and talents that He has given us.

Recognizing that all of us are truly ordinary people, each of us can accept the challenge from this family to make a difference that will last forever for people in the world in which we live. That would be the prayer of Ben and Ruth.

May this book encourage you to make such a difference as you focus your L.I.F.E. on serving others. May your prayer walks keep you focused.

—Dick Abel, Brig. Gen., USAF (Ret.)

TABLE OF CONTENTS

Thanks...v
Foreword...vii

SPECIAL AGENT BEN:
How I Became an Improbable Special Agent.................1

    Decisions / Decisions 3
    Smoking the Peace Pipe 7
    Kicking off the Second Half...............................11
    Prayer Walking 12
    From Success to Significance 17
    The L.I.F.E. Principle 20

1ST ASSIGNMENT: "L" IS FOR LABOR
Special Agent Ben's Assignment to Mongolia 25

    Kublai Khan Asks for Teachers.............................26
    Is This Crazy or What?....................................32
    A Cast of Characters......................................34
    Tom Questions the Vice President 36
    Fly the Friendly Skies of MIAT............................38
    The Longest Ride..42
    If This Isn't the End of the Earth........................46
    Hot Tub Heaven..49
    Good News, Bad News 51
    The Mongolian Barbecue....................................54
    Thieves, Thugs & Bandits..................................57
    Don't You Love It When a Plan Comes Together! 59
    Window from Heaven..61
    Farewell to the Mayor.....................................64

Don't Do Anything Stupid! 66
The Heart of a Teacher. 69
A Few Parting Thoughts 73
Hot Off the Press. 75

2ND ASSIGNMENT: "I" IS FOR INFLUENCE
Special Agent Ben's Assignment to Russia 83

What on Earth is "INFLUENCE"?. 84
The General's Invitation. 86
A Special Party-Mix Team. 88
Touring the Kremlin. 90
Can I Add This to My Resume?. 94
"Star City" and Cosmonaut Volkov 96
Seminar at the Nuclear Missile Base 99
Pickled Garlic Cloves & Vodka 102
The Power of Influence. 105
To Bless or Be Blessed: That is the Question!. 107
Mandi and her Spinning Wheels. 111

3RD ASSIGNMENT: "F" IS FOR FINANCES
Special Agent Ben's Assignment to China 119

A MAJOR Challenge. 120
A Family Treasure Lost for Fifty Years 125
The China Team!. 130
One Miserable Singaporean! 132
Jet Lag & the Upside-Down Clock 134
Esther & the Miracles 136
Searching for Lost Family Treasure 140
A Powerful Prayer. 142
The Liver-Shaker Ride 144
A Divine Appointment. 147

FOUND: A Lost Family Treasure......................149
How to Blow Away an Aunt...........................154
The Rag-Tag Team 157
A White-Haired Grandma Goes to Hong Kong 161
James Chu: The Hamburger Man 166
Cramming Seven Days into Seven Hours 169
The Great Reunion 171
That Dam Project & the Wanzhou Church Split........173
How It Feels to Be a Rock Star 175
101 Ways to Wok Your Dog 178
Devil City...181
Grandma Gets Her Gift 184

4TH ASSIGNMENT: "E" IS FOR EXPERTISE
Special Agent Ben's Assignment to Colombia *193*

Forrest Gump or Indiana Jones?.....................194
Sure, I'd Like to Visit Juan Valdez 196
A Strange & Funny Meeting 198
Running the Gauntlet at the Colombian Airport......205
Drug Hit Man, a.k.a. Our Body Guard 208
A Plan Unfolds.....................................211
Leaving Our Hearts in Colombia 217
Journal Notes & Quotes 219
You Want Me to Speak in Colombia?..................223
Total Success 4x2..................................226
My Competitive Advantage: Four Keys to Success 228
A Heart is Changed.................................234
Two Qualities of Leadership that Money Can't Buy ..236
Pep Rally 101 244

THE L.I.F.E. OF A SPECIAL AGENT
Special Agent 'You': Assignment to the World 253

    How to Develop Your Eternal Business Plan. 254

    Pros & Cons of Overseas Missions 256

    What Can You Expect?. 259

    Time Management 101 262

    Why Do You Give?. 265

    Why Do You Do What You Do?. 269

    The Great Disconnect. 272

    Finishing Strong 275

    The Book of L.I.F.E. 279

    My Special Agent L.I.F.E. Journal 280

    SQJ—Stories, Questions, and Journaling 284

APPENDICES

    Appendix A: The Lord's Prayer. 312

    Appendix B: Four Daily Disciplines that
                    Lead to Personal Success. 315

    Appendix C: Favorite Quotes. 317

    Appendix D: Register Here for
                    Special Agent Opportunities 320

SQJ—STORIES, QUESTIONS, AND JOURNALING

S. **STORIES** *create a memorable way of learning new ideas through someone else's experience.*

Q. **QUESTIONS** *lead us to wrestle with new ideas and process what they really mean.*

J. **JOURNALING** *helps us imagine how those ideas might look in our own lives.*

In order to get the most out of the stories in the book, we recommend answering the questions which are listed at the end of the book. Perfect for small-group discussion or personal journaling, these questions highlight the transferable concepts that inspire personal growth and transformational learning in your own life. ***Let the adventure begin!***

SPECIAL AGENT BEN:

How I Became an Improbable Special Agent

DATE: June 1992
LOCATION: Mountains of Mongolia
EVENT: A Wild Decision

DECISIONS / DECISIONS

Don't do anything stupid? I had no choice!
I had to do something stupid.

◆ ◆ ◆

We had boarded the plane and taxied halfway down the Mongolian meadow airstrip when the pilot saw a shepherd leading his flock across the field in front of us. He veered off the hard-packed grass to miss the sheep and the wheels slipped into the soggy soil and sank.

We unloaded the passengers and the luggage, then shoveled mud out from under the tires while the pilot revved his engines. The plane moved five feet. We dug some more, he revved the engines again and 1 ½ hours after the mishap, the plane was finally back on solid ground. By now, the sheep were long gone.

The pilot looked up at the sky and said, "You see that thunderhead at the end of the meadow? If we wait for the storm to pass and this field gets any wetter, we will be grounded for days. It's now or never. Get on!"

We were running to the plane when I suddenly remembered Nancy's parting words, "Ben, while you're in Mongolia, just remember you've got a wife and three kids at home. Don't do anything stupid!"

In that instant, it was as though time stood still. My mind flashed back…

- *We've just wasted 1 ½ hours' worth of fuel revving the engines*
- *The plane is overloaded: three people per every two seats, plus goats and bundles of freight*
- *The airstrip is wet and slow*
- *We're taking off into a thunderhead*
- *How do I follow Nancy's advice?*
- *Getting on that plane is stupid*
- *Riding horseback over the mountains for 40 days eating old mutton is stupid*
- *If only Nancy could understand… It's not a matter of not doing something stupid. It's a matter of choosing which stupid thing I'm about to do is less stupid than the other stupid thing I'm about to do.*

Either option could kill me! Given the choices and the limited time to decide, I said a quick prayer and ran for the plane. I thought: *If I'm gonna die, I might as well go fast.*

How on earth did I ever get myself into such a tense situation? I've heard it said that when you're in a near-death crisis, your whole life flashes before you. In that instant, I saw all the significant events leading up to this moment—growing up in my childhood home, meeting my mate and raising our three children, building my business career, becoming an improbable special agent, and finding myself in this crazy predicament in Mongolia.

◆ ◆ ◆

My name is Ben Manthei (mŏn-tie), and I was born into a family of business entrepreneurs. Hard work and biblical values led my father and his brother to achieve success first in strawberry farming and later in veneer manufacturing. I grew up in this atmosphere of success.

I was the youngest son in a family of five boys and two girls and our parents raised us with strong Christian values. During college, I decided to embrace Christianity as my own, which set my course for life. I also met my delightful wife, Nancy, and after finishing school, I invested all my energy into my career and family.

I experienced financial success early on, having teamed up with my older siblings in a number of business ventures, including a veneer manufacturing plant and a concrete/aggregate/underground construction business. Together with our cousins, my brothers and I built several resort parks in California, along with housing developments in Michigan and Nevada. Mid-career, I founded Redi-Rock Int. (a large block retaining wall system franchise), which grew to over 200 licensed manufactures and expanded to over 40 countries. For fun, we dabbled in miscellaneous investments like "drive-through" coffee shops and motion picture production.

Despite our business successes, I knew deep inside that there was more to life than making money. About the time I reached mid-life, we encountered a group of people who invested not only their money but their lives into endeavors with eternal significance. These men challenged us to develop an eternal business plan, which opened the door to a whole new L.I.F.E. of adventure. L.I.F.E. is an acronym for Labor, Influence, Finances, and Expertise.

The L.I.F.E. Principle is both the story and the challenge that I would like to share. Each assignment led to new people and places—people like the mayor of Uliastai in places like Mongolia, and strange predicaments with surprising results.

WARNING: Proceed with caution.
This book could change your L.I.F.E.!

DATE: Spring 1975
LOCATION: Bethany Lutheran College
EVENT: Saturday Night Bull Session

SMOKING THE PEACE PIPE

I peered at Dean through the blue haze. Could he be serious?

It was a typical Friday night and the guys on our floor had met for a bull session in our dorm room after dropping off their dates at the girls' dorm before the midnight curfew. We smoked our pipes and told stories, and when the other guys left, Dean and I kicked back to finish our last smoke. That's when Dean turned to me and said something that profoundly impacted my life.

Before I tell you what he said, it's important that you understand a bit about our backgrounds.

I was a fun-loving kid whose greatest downfall was pulling practical jokes on my friends and harassing my little sister, Ruth. You see, I was raised in a home where God was as real as my parents. We prayed at every meal and supper always ended with a mini-church service of Bible reading, prayer, and a hymn. It didn't matter what any of us seven kids had planned for the evening, no one went anywhere until we'd finished devotions.

As you can imagine, we always went to church on Sunday.

Dean, on the other hand, was an atheist. He had experienced it all… wine, women, and song. He came to Bethany because he had been recruited to play basketball. Dean was tall and blond, the life of the party, and every girl's heartthrob. I had been elected Homecoming King that year, but Dean was still "the Dream!"

Although our backgrounds were opposite, Dean and I had one thing in common. We were both looking for adventure in life. We were experimenting to see what worked, what was important, and what values we would choose to build our lives upon. Dean took me to the bars on Friday night, and I took him to church on Sunday.

Unlike most students on campus, Dean and I both had wheels. In fact, we had both owned cars since our junior years in high school. We wondered what it was like for the other students who had to catch rides, so one weekend we decided to leave our cars behind and hitchhike to Minneapolis to visit Dean's friend. When we arrived in the city on Friday night, his friend wasn't home yet, so we sat on the embankment of his front lawn and watched the neighbors come home from their dates. One pretty gal who lived next door kissed her boyfriend goodbye and stopped on the way up the sidewalk to ask what we were doing.

Dean was quick to respond. "Oh, we're just waiting for my friend."

She asked where we were from and when we said, "Bethany College in Mankato," her eyes lit up.

"I've been thinking about going there next year! Is that a good school?"

"Absolutely," Dean said. "I would recommend Bethany to anyone. It's changed my life. I used to be an atheist and now I'm agnostic."

I thought, *Whoa! What kind of a recommendation is that?*

Now it was a year later, and we were smoking our pipes when Dean stunned me with his announcement. "Ben, I made a major decision today. I have turned my life over to Christ and things are going to be different!"

Could he be serious? I wondered. Dean had experienced all the world had to offer—things I had only dreamed of doing but never had the guts to try. Now he was chucking it all for the kind of life I had grown up with.

He told me about the hurts he had experienced as a result of his free-wheeling lifestyle. He explained that his girlfriend had been sharing Jesus with him, he knew he was a sinner, and he had asked Jesus to come into his life. He was forgiven, clean, and starting on a new journey.

In the following months, I watched in fascination as Dean truly became a different person. I had never seen with my own eyes the power of the gospel to transform a life, and this was not just any life but that of my roommate, "Dean the Dream!"

Someone once warned me that three major decisions would determine the entire course of my life: the god I chose to serve would become my Master, the woman I chose to love would become my Mate, and the career I chose to pursue would become my Mission. He urged me to choose wisely.

As I watched Dean choose his "Master" and allow Jesus to

direct his life, I was challenged to search my own soul. I had always believed in Jesus, but was I willing to let Him be my Master?

Dean and I approached the question from opposite directions, but I eventually arrived at the same conclusion as he did. On a bright spring day after a stirring chapel service, I returned to our dorm room and wrote the following words in the back of my Bible:

"I have decided to follow Jesus. No turning back!"

Little did I know that this decision would open the door to an incredible life of adventure.

DATE: February 1995
LOCATION: My House
EVENT: Fireside Contemplations

KICKING OFF THE SECOND HALF

The Big 4-0! I had just celebrated my 40th birthday and was reflecting on life as I sat in the living room and gazed into the fire. I thought: *Since many people live to be eighty, I've hit the half-way point.* Now I was officially middle-aged.

As I reviewed the first half of my life, I felt very blessed. I had finished school, married my lovely wife Nancy, had three wonderful children, a beautiful home, and built several businesses with my brothers and cousins. I had experienced success in many ways and was pleased with the way I had invested my energies over the years.

Then I asked myself: *What do I want to do with the second half of my life? Twenty years from now, what do I want my life to look like? Do I want to work hard so our businesses will double or triple in size? Is that all there is? Or could there be something more?*

"Something more." My mind latched onto that thought. If there was something more to experience, I was determined to discover it!

DATE: 1996
LOCATION: Pontiac Silverdome
EVENT: Promise Keepers

PRAYER WALKING

"Prayer Walking"? What on earth is that?

I was surrounded by 60,000 men at a Promise Keepers event in the Pontiac Silverdome, listening intently to a dynamic motivational speaker and thinking, *I wish I'd brought Steve. He really needs to hear this.* The next point made me think of John. *Oh, he really needs to hear this!* I had been a Christian for many years and had somehow slipped into an attitude of thinking there was nothing new for me to learn.

Suddenly, the speaker made a point that hit me over the head like a sledgehammer and I thought, *I know who needs to hear this. It's me! I need to make some major changes in my life.*

I cannot tell you exactly what he said. Although I may hear what a speaker is saying, I only remember what the Holy Spirit speaks to my heart through the message. Whatever he said made me ask myself some tough questions:

How much time do I invest each day into building up my relationships? How much time do I devote to my wife and children? How much time do I devote to God? Do I schedule a time into each day when I deliberately honor them with my full attention?

As I pondered those questions, I started to slink down in my seat. I had never disciplined myself to spend deliberate quality time with anyone.

When the speaker told us about his exciting daily discipline of "Prayer Walking," I knew I wanted to try it. I needed the exercise, and I needed to spend more time in prayer. This was just the perfect plan.

The night I returned home, I set my alarm clock thirty minutes earlier than usual for the following day so I could get up and walk before work. Then I asked God to be with me in this new endeavor. The first few days were hard, but by the second week I went to bed looking forward to my morning Prayer Walks.

Here's how Prayer Walking works. It's like scheduling a daily appointment with God. Each morning before I head to work, I go for a walk and pray through the Lord's Prayer, making each section personal to me as I walk. By the time I finish, I've talked with God about every important area of my life. *(See Appendix A: The Lord's Prayer)*

I live in the country at the top of a hill. I began Prayer Walking one mile to the lake at the end of the road and back, up and down several hills. One winter morning, a skiff of snow had covered the road and as I reached the bottom of the hill, my feet shot out from under me, and I landed flat on my back in a puddle at the end of the neighbor's driveway. Although the water was only inches deep, I was completely soaked from my shoulders to my knees.

I said, "Lord, why did this happen? Here I am honoring You on my Prayer Walk…"

Then I realized that we live in a dual world. The physical realm is very real. It's a fallen world, and if I fall in the water, I get wet. But the spiritual world is just as real.

I remembered a story I had read in a book called *Primary Purpose*, by Ted Haggard. He related an event experienced by the men who started Prayer Walking. They'd been meeting in the basement of one of their homes and found their minds wandering as they prayed. So, they decided to get up and walk around town, praying for the people and places they passed. One day they decided to walk around the hospital. When they reached the front door, they felt led to go inside and walk the halls of the hospital. Before long they came to the OB unit and stopped to admire the newborns. Suddenly the eyes of one of the men were opened to see into the spirit realm and he saw a group of demons hovering over the cribs. He watched the head demon assign a demon of greed to one baby and to another a demon of lust. The next little baby received a demon of anger. It shocked the man, and he said, "This is wrong! This should not be happening!" The two men asked God to push back the demonic powers through the blood of Jesus. As soon as they spoke the name of JESUS, the demons fled. Then, when the men began to pray blessings over the babies, angels appeared! The head angel assigned an angel of peace to one baby, an angel of contentment to another, and an angel of joy to a third. The next little baby was given an angel of love. The men then remembered the Bible verse that states:

"We do not wrestle against flesh and blood but principalities and spiritual powers in high places" (Ephesians 6:12).

The spirit realm is every bit as real as the physical world. When I fell into the mud puddle and got wet, that was reality in the physical realm. When the men prayed for those babies, that was reality in the spiritual realm.

During my Prayer Walks, I learned to wrestle against the spiritual forces that influenced my world. God brought thoughts to my mind that never would have occurred to me if I had not taken the time to walk and pray. As I prayed about my relationship with my wife, Nancy, I saw specific areas I needed to change. The same thing happened as I prayed about my relationships with our children: Lindsey, Andy, and Jacob. God even gave me specific insights for that day's meetings and relationships at work. Phenomenal things! Sometimes I would pray for the people I had met in my travels and, before I knew it, I was half-a-world away… and then surprised to find myself back at my own driveway. I'd think, *I'm home already?* My prayer time had been that exciting.

When summer arrived, I had been Prayer Walking for about six months and decided to change my route to walk on a trail through the woods. One day I got to the part of the Lord's Prayer that says, "Hallowed be Thy name," and I began praying, "Holy, holy, holy, Lord God of Hosts… who was with the patriarchs of old, who is with us today, and who is to come, when one day every knee shall bow and every tongue confess that Jesus Christ is Lord…" As I worshipped, I suddenly felt the presence of God come down on me in a way I had never experienced before, and

I burst into tears. I couldn't stop weeping—for the entire walk. I sensed God's holiness and was completely undone. The only thing I could do was confess sin. There was no arguing. No room for pride. When I got home, I knew that I had just developed a personal friendship with my Creator. He had met me in a special way to confirm that I'm not alone when I set aside these times between us. He honors our appointments.

Thanks to the challenge of that speaker at the Promise Keepers event, prayer walking has become one of my most cherished daily disciplines. It enabled me to develop an intimate relationship with the living God of the universe, a relationship of trust where I can talk to Him about everything in my life, big or small. I also gained a whole new sense of anticipation to listen for God's still small voice speaking to me, which enriched each day and prepared me for a whole new level of adventure in my life.

DATE: 1997
LOCATION: Washington DC
EVENT: A Significant Conference

FROM SUCCESS TO SIGNIFICANCE

The Quest for Significance.
What a tantalizing title for a conference!

The brochure intrigued me with the question, "*What is the difference between Success and Significance?*" I had no answer to that question in my own life, so I was curious to hear what the speakers might have to say. I mailed in my registration fee and packed my bags.

The conference covered some fascinating topics that helped me begin to sense what "something more" might be that could be added to the second half of my life.

The speakers posed some penetrating questions and shared profound perspectives. What if you were to become the richest person in the whole world, only to lose your own soul? Wouldn't that be a tragedy? It certainly wouldn't be a success! The world's definition of success involves money, fame, and power. We all know people who have achieved a great deal of worldly success in their careers as athletes, musicians, politicians, businessmen, and actors. But along the way, we have also seen people who achieved worldly success and didn't know how to handle it. They ultimately squandered their riches or lost themselves in addictions. This leaves one to wonder: *Is success all there is? Or could there be some transcending virtue that transforms success into significance?*

The virtue which leads to true significance begins with a heart ready to listen and a spirit willing to obey. Those two keys open the door for us to see God's mighty hand working through our lives in a way that will last for eternity.

Eternity? What am I doing today that will make a difference a thousand years from now?

As I pondered that question, I could only think of three things that would last forever. We can't do anything about two of these.

- God says HE will last forever, but we cannot change that.
- God says HIS WORD will last forever, but we cannot change that.
- God says the SOULS of people will last forever, and we can influence where those souls will spend eternity.

Unlike the things we work so hard to acquire but which will ultimately vanish, the souls of our friends will last forever. But where will they live? Will they be with God enjoying His love forever? Or will they spend eternity separated from the One who loves them most? We have the incredible privilege of touching people in a way that will have an eternal impact on their lives by sharing the saving message of eternal life through Jesus Christ.

Many people have never even heard the name of Jesus!

When the conference ended, I came away with a new understanding of the difference between success and significance.

- Success is the reward you gain from being very good at what you do.
- Significance is using your success to make a difference for eternity.
- True significance is not doing great things for God, but rather, allowing God to accomplish His goals through you.

My Prayer Walks took on a new dimension after that. I began to ask God what I might do in my life today that would make a difference for eternity. How could I allow Him to accomplish His goals through me? Those prayers led me to wonder: *What might He ask me to do? What if I don't like it?* This prompted me to pray also that He would give me courage to obey whatever He might ask me to do.

I had no idea how much excitement I would have as God began to answer those prayers!

Date: 1997
Location: Breckenridge, Colorado
Event: World Briefing

THE L.I.F.E. PRINCIPLE

"God doesn't want your money. He wants your life!"
That statement hit me like a 2x4 across my head.

Four family members were seated at the table listening to Dave Hannah speak from the podium. This conference was the annual World Briefing of Campus Crusade for Christ, where staff leaders share personal glimpses into the exciting things God is doing around the world. We had been invited to this event by a businessman who was a member of "History's Handful"—a group of people committed to making a major financial investment during their lifetime to help fulfill the Great Commission to make disciples of all nations and help shape history.

We understood that we would be challenged to team up with this ministry, but I never expected anything so drastic. *God doesn't want my money? He wants my life?* Hannah went on to explain that L.I.F.E is an acronym.

L *is for Labor*
I *is for Influence*
F *is for Finances*
E *is for Expertise*

He then challenged each of us to consider how we might invest our L.I.F.E. in such a way that would positively impact people's souls for all eternity. He also urged us to evaluate our business goals to see how they fit into this picture. I thought: *Now, that would be an eternal business plan! What a dynamic concept! But what would it look like in real life? In our business? How could it apply to my L.I.F.E.?*

For the next two years, I prayed about the L.I.F.E. principle on my daily prayer walks. How might God use my particular mix of gifts and skills? How could I utilize my Labor, Influence, Finances, and Expertise for God's Kingdom?

I was soaking in our hot tub one night when, suddenly, the light bulb flashed, and the picture clicked into focus. *I had already seen the L.I.F.E. Principle lived out in real life—my life—for the past seven years!* I had used my Labor in Mongolia, my Influence in Russia, my Finances in China, and my Expertise in Colombia.

My moment of epiphany was so inspiring that I told my wife, "Nancy, I need to write a book!" She shook her head and said, "Ben, you've come up with some great ideas in the hot tub, but this time I think you cooked your brains too long! You haven't even *read* a book since college. How are you ever going to *write* one now?" Nancy was right. I realized I wasn't a writer. But then

I remembered that my sister, Ruth, was a writer! So, we decided to team up and share the exciting discoveries God has taught us as a family.

This tale could be told by more qualified people who have even better stories to tell. Yet, for some reason, God has laid it on our hearts to share these stories with you. I thoroughly enjoy the excitement of a good Indiana Jones movie, but there's nothing like experiencing an incredible adventure yourself. What a thrill! Who knows? This challenge may even open a new door in your own L.I.F.E. adventure!

Smoking the Peace Pipe
- Our College Days
*Dean the Dream, Ben,
Dave, Jim*

The Ben Manthei Family
*Ben, Nancy, Jacob,
Lindsey, Andy*

1ST ASSIGNMENT—
"L" is for Labor

Special Agent Ben's Assignment to Mongolia

Your assignment, should you choose to accept it, is to take time out of your busy schedule to go to Mongolia and use your Labor to prepare the way for future teachers to use their Labor in the remote town of Uliastai.

You will be part of a small reconnaissance team who will determine whether or not conditions are livable and if it is wise to send teachers to that town.

You will be escorted by Paul Hogan, President of ELIC.

Assignment to Mongolia

1st ASSIGNMENT: "L" IS FOR LABOR

Special Agent Ben's Assignment to Mongolia

Date: 1991
Location: My House
Event: After-Dinner Discussion

KUBLAI KHAN ASKS FOR TEACHERS

As usual Nancy had outdone herself with a fabulous dinner. Afterward, we settled into comfortable chairs in the living room where we could put our feet up. I thought: *The conversation had better be lively if I'm going to stay awake with this contented stomach!*

Tom wasted no time getting to the point. "What have you got, Hogan? You flew all the way from California to tell us about Mongolia. This must be good." Fun-loving and enthusiastic, Hogan was one of those missionaries my family loved to entertain. My cousin and comrade in living on the cutting edge, Tom, and I had met him through mutual friends and found ourselves intrigued with his approach. Hogan was the director of a ministry that mobilized English teachers and sent them to developing nations to share the love of Jesus through friendships while teaching the English language. Tonight, the sparkle in his eye indicated that he had us right where he wanted us.

"Gentlemen, what I'm about to share with you is a

once-in-a-lifetime opportunity. How much do you know about Mongolia?"

We shook our heads in unison. "Not much!"

"Well, does the name Genghis Khan ring any bells?"

I nodded. "I heard his name in school once upon a time."

"Well, I think you'll find his story fascinating in light of the opportunity that stands before us."

"You're kidding, right?" Tom said. "How could Genghis Khan have anything to do with us?"

Hogan laughed. "Oh, you'd be surprised. He's been dead about 800 years, but by the time I've finished this story I think you'll be amazed at the connection."

Suddenly I didn't feel the least bit sleepy. He had my full attention.

"In the early 1200s, Genghis Khan and his Mongolian hordes conquered the entire continent of Asia. Their empire spread from Eastern Europe to the Pacific Ocean and from Russia down through Persia. In fact, the land under his rule was larger than the Roman Empire."

Tom's eyes widened. "I didn't realize he was that powerful!"

"That's what makes this next part so incredible. Two generations later, during the Golden years of the Mongolian Empire, his grandson, Kublai Khan, met Marco Polo's father who was traveling through Mongolia on business in the year 1266. They must have had a fascinating conversation because Kublai Khan asked Polo to deliver the following message to the governing Christians in Rome:

"Send to me 100 teachers of the Christian faith who are able to clearly show that the laws of Christ are best. If persuaded, I and all under my rule will become his followers."

I sat up straighter in my chair. "What an incredible opportunity to influence an entire empire!"

Hogan nodded. "You're getting the picture. Kublai Khan was the most powerful ruler on earth and his request for 100 Christian teachers was an opportunity unparalleled in history. Can you imagine what might have happened if those teachers had gone to Mongolia?"

"You mean they never went?" Tom asked. Hogan shook his head. "Why, that's unbelievable! How on earth could they ignore such a request?"

"Polo found only two teachers who were willing to go. They set out on their journey but were forced to return to Rome because they were unprepared for the rugged Himalayas' harsh conditions. Kublai Khan's request was never fulfilled, and the message they were invited to bring to Mongolia never reached the hearts of the people at the 'ends of the earth.' "

"That's tragic!" I said.

"What's sadder yet is that Kublai Khan didn't give up. He was determined to establish a new religion among his people, so he sent the same challenge to the Buddhists of Tibet requesting 100 Buddhist teachers. They fulfilled his request and as a result, Asia is now steeped in Buddhism. Not only did the message of Christ not reach the heart of Kublai Khan, but the entire continent of

Asia has remained lost to the life-changing truth of Jesus Christ and has floundered in spiritual darkness for the past eight centuries. At the turn of the 20th century, Mongolia was considered the most "religious" nation on earth because of their deep hunger for spiritual things. In 1924, the Soviets invaded Mongolia with their atheistic communism and stripped them of their culture and religion. They wounded the hearts of Mongolians more during their 70 years of suppression than anything else the people had ever suffered."

I said, "That's depressing! I thought you said this was going to be an exciting story."

"It is. I'm just getting to the good part. Remember when the Berlin Wall came down?"

Of course we remembered.

"Well, even though the media never mentioned it, the same thing happened in Mongolia. The Mongolian people won the right for free democratic elections and elected a new reformed government. The younger generation no longer wants Russian as their second language. Instead, they want to study English so they can interact with the modern world."

Tom and I looked at each other and nodded. We both had an inkling where this was going.

"Here's the clincher. The Mongolian Ministry of Education contacted me last month to see if we would consider sending English teachers into Mongolia. Next month, I'll meet with the Prime Minister and the Vice President. Do you see what's happening here? It's like the request of Kublai Khan all over again.

When they asked me to send English teachers, they're really asking for teachers who can share the love of Jesus Christ!

"Men, right now the hearts of the Mongolian people are very open to friendships with North Americans. This means that we have the opportunity to impact this entire generation of Mongolians! I know your desire to get involved with worthy mission ventures, so I wanted to share this incredible opportunity with you. If ever there was a moment for the light of truth to shine into Mongolia, this is it. Just as the great Kublai Khan asked Rome to send them 100 Christian teachers over 700 years ago, the government of Mongolia is now asking *us* to send them English teachers.

"I am determined that this time, by the grace of God, when 100 caring Christian teachers journey to Mongolia to share their language and their Lord with this generation, there will be no turning back. Mongolia has been in the shadows long enough. This time, the light of the gospel will rise in the hearts of those who are living at the 'ends of the earth.'"

"Where do we fit in, Hogan?" I asked.

"Tom... Ben... I'd like you to come with me to Mongolia next month when I meet with the government leaders and see for yourselves what is happening. You would be hard pressed to find a ministry opportunity as significant, urgent, and timely as this."

Tom and I studied each other for a moment. Then I remembered my schedule. "Hogan, I can't go next month. We've got way too many jobs going on at work."

"I understand. Well then, would you come with me nine

months from now when I travel to Uliastai, Mongolia, and prepare the way to send in teachers?"

Tom and I looked at each other and shrugged. We didn't have a clue what we'd be doing nine months from now, so we said, "Maybe we could go in nine months. That might work."

I was thinking: *Nine months is a long time off. He'll forget all about us by then.*

Hogan grabbed our hands and raised them into the air. "Mongolia, here we come!" We all laughed.

Hogan went back to California the next day, and Mongolia completely left my mind. So, a week later, I was surprised when Tom and I received two airline tickets to Mongolia dated nine months from the day Hogan had visited my home. He included a little note that said, "These tickets are non-refundable. I know you guys are too conservative to let them go to waste. Mongolia, here we come!"

He knew us well. We were going to Mongolia.

```
Date:     June 29, 1992
Location: O'Hare Airport, Chicago
Event:    Flying to Mongolia
```

IS THIS CRAZY OR WHAT?

Nine months later, Tom and I found ourselves sitting in O'Hare Airport on our way to Mongolia.

We'd flown from Traverse City, Michigan, down to Chicago, where we would catch our international flight to Tokyo, where we were scheduled to meet Hogan and the others. We would all travel together to Beijing, and then on to Ulaanbaatar, the capital of Mongolia.

We were waiting for our flight when I looked at Tom and said, "Is this crazy or what? We have so much work at home. Here we are flying to Mongolia, and I don't even know where it is! I haven't thought a thing about Mongolia. Why are we doing this?"

Tom said, "We're doing this because Hogan asked us to go, and we want to help him out." It was as simple as that.

I looked down at my ticket and started to pray. "Lord, I have no idea why we are going to Mongolia. If You want me to get involved personally, then You need to change my heart, because right now, I have no love in my heart for these people."

Once I was honest with God about how I felt, I could think of other things to pray for:

- I asked God to help me see the people in Mongolia from His perspective.
- I prayed for a vision of how we could impact Mongolia with God's love and that God would give me some of His love for those people.
- I prayed for God to free me from my concerns, worries, and self-pity so I could see ways to help others.
- I asked God to be with Nancy, Jacob, Lindsey, and Andy while I was away, to comfort, protect and encourage them.

Then I wrote in my journal…

I feel renewed and excited, anticipating what I may learn next as I ask God to take full control of whatever circumstances we might encounter.

When it came time for departure, we learned that the boarding ramp had damaged the hinges so the airplane's door couldn't close properly, and our flight was delayed. I thought: *We still have time to back out!* Just then Tom turned to me and said, "If my wife, Teri, were here, she would say, 'This is a sign we're not to go.' But Teri's not here, and we're going!"

Three hours later, the parts arrived from Seattle, and we were off to Mongolia.

Date: July 1992
Location: Mongolia

A CAST OF CHARACTERS

HOGAN & COMPANY

Hogan, our Hero	President and Founder of ELIC
Phil Hubbard	Board member of ELIC Former owner of a stock exchange company
Patsy Hubbard	Wife of Phil, kept a detailed diary of the journey
Bob Foster	Chairman of the Board of ELIC. Owner of a dude ranch in Colorado
Marion Foster	Wife of Bob, encouraged teachers

ULAANBAATAR, MONGOLIA

VP Gonchigdo	Vice President of Mongolia
Mashbileg	Interpreter during negotiations with government officials
Eredene	Traveling interpreter (a.k.a. 'Air Dan')
Ron Forseth & family	Career teacher with ELIC, newly assigned to Mongolia
Karla Johnson	One-Year teacher, MIT graduate who designed jet engines

ULIASTAI, MONGOLIA

Mayor Harla	Mayor of Uliastai
Drivers	Drove van and jeep, saved my lure in the river

THE MONGOLIAN RESORT

"Church Mouse" and her two friends	Chambermaids who tucked us in at night
Old military man Cook	78-year-old veteran of two wars against Japan. Served us fermented yak milk and old mutton
Butcher	Performed ceremonial slaughter of the sheep for our feast

Date: July 1992
Location: Parliament Building
Event: Meeting with Vice President

TOM QUESTIONS THE VICE PRESIDENT

Tom was never at a loss for words—that's what made this moment so remarkable.

Officially, this was our most important day in Mongolia. Hogan was meeting with Vice President Gonchigdo to present him with the first English textbooks published exclusively for the Mongolian people. These textbooks would be used in all secondary schools throughout the entire nation. A movie camera and photographer had joined us for the historical event and the atmosphere was hushed and formal.

We were led to the inner sanctum of the Parliament building and seated at a very long conference table. The Mongolian officials sat along one side of the table with the Americans opposite them. After introductions were made, Hogan began negotiating with the Vice President through Mashbileg, our interpreter.

Tom and I were seated at the farthest end of the table—much too far to hear the conversation. Eventually we became bored and started whispering to pass the time.

Have you ever been in that situation in class where you were talking with a friend and your mind was really far away, when suddenly the teacher asked you a question? If so, you can imagine how Tom felt when, without warning, Hogan leaned forward until he could see us at the far end of the table and said loudly, "Tom, do you have a question for the Vice President?"

Tom was stunned. For once in his life, Tom had no words to say!

I found this incredibly amusing. Having been in business with Tom and seen his power of persuasion at the negotiating table, this was a historical moment in our lives. It was also a moment Tom would not live down. For the rest of the trip, every few hours he would hear, "Tom, do you have a question for the Vice President?"

We both learned a valuable lesson from that experience. When you go to a foreign country and meet with dignitaries, be prepared to converse. Always have a question or a word of praise on the tip of your tongue. Fortunately for us, Bob jumped in with a few words to smooth over the situation. He was prepared, and it will be a long time before Tom is ever caught with his proverbial "pants down" again.

Date: July 1992
Location: Ulaanbaatar, Mongolia
Event: Flight to Uliastai

FLY THE FRIENDLY SKIES OF MIAT

I'd never seen a riot before. Pushing and shoving. I counted fifteen fights!

The airport seemed normal when we arrived in Ulaanbaatar on our international flight, but now we discovered that domestic flights were another story. MIAT was the only domestic airline in Mongolia, and they were in the midst of a crisis situation.

The airport bus had just delivered us to our plane, a vintage 1950 Russian two-engine prop plane that seated about 40 people. To our consternation, an enormous crowd was on the tarmac waiting to board. Uniformed officers were attempting to hold back the crowd while passengers disembarked. When the last one reached the bottom step, everyone rushed forward. We stayed a good distance away and watched "Air Dan" wiggle his way to the front of the crowd to show our tickets to the flight personnel. We had paid many times the price of any of the locals and saw that most of the crowd had no tickets at all. At Air Dan's signal, we made our way to the plane. Being Americans in a third-world country is a mixed bag. We were overcharged, but we were also the first to board.

Just as we took our seats, a riot broke out as the rest of the crowd stormed the plane. Hogan had instructed us to sit near the back for ventilation, and it was a great place to watch the action. A couple of guys heaved people out of their way so they could crawl up the steps, only to be confronted by two husky stewardesses who shoved them back out the door because they had no tickets. These ladies were not the "smiling faces on the friendly skies of United!" One guy climbed back in, and she bounced him out so hard he missed the steps and fell straight down to the tarmac. He got up and sneaked in three more times. The last time I saw him was when they pulled him out of the luggage compartment.

The day was hot—90 degrees in the shade and hotter on the tarmac. As passengers piled in, it grew so stuffy that people fainted. I was very grateful to be sitting by the door. When the flight attendants finally decided the aircraft was full, there were three people packed into every two seats, along with goats and bundles of freight.

The engines roared into action, and when the air conditioners came on, they blew white stuff into the plane until the air got so foggy, I could barely see in front of me.

I looked around to survey the situation. The overloaded plane filled with fog did not look safe to me and I wanted off! I lobbied with the others to convince Hogan to bail out, but they were too stunned to reply. Finally, I went directly to our fearless leader.

"Hogan, this does not look safe. Maybe we should reconsider…"

Hogan looked me straight in the eye and said, "Ben, do you really think I would ask you to do anything unsafe with Nancy, Andy, Lindsey, and Jacob at home? Do you think that I would ask you to do anything unsafe?"

We looked around the plane and burst into laughter. It was ludicrous! Hogan's knack for the ridiculous diffused my tension. Before the day was out, I would see that his sense of humor was truly a gift from God. The door slammed shut, our decision was made, and we were on our way.

Although MIAT has the highest crash ratio of any airline in the world, we had an uneventful 2 ½-hour flight to the middle of nowhere and landed on a dirt strip in a desolate meadow surrounded by mountains. I saw one open building with a rusty generator inside and thought: *This is Uliastai?* We deplaned, gathered our luggage from the grass, and watched our fellow passengers wander away in every direction into the mountains until we were the only ones left.

We just stood there, holding our luggage, and looking around the empty meadow. I'd never felt so lost in my life. Finally, someone asked, "What do we do now?" Hogan put on his characteristic grin, pointed to the horizon. We all squinted, looking in that direction, when we saw a distant caravan of Russian army jeeps heading our way.

By the time they arrived, I'd gone into shock—culture shock! Our six-day trip included traveling in America, Japan, China, and Mongolia. I'd experienced jet lag, unfamiliar Asian food, pungent odors, and the chaos of our MIAT flight. I couldn't take any more surprises. I needed to go home, and I'd only just arrived at the "ends of the earth."

Hogan introduced us to "the mayor of Uliastai" who had come to pick us up, and I thought: *Big deal, the mayor of Uliastai. What is Uliastai? A derelict building in the middle of nowhere!*

Little did I know that in the days ahead the mayor of Uliastai would become a significant person in my life. God had a plan for answering my O'Hare Airport prayer. But at this moment, I just wanted out!

```
Date: July 4th, 1992
Location: Central Mongolia
Event: Trip to the Mongolian Resort
```

THE LONGEST RIDE

Culture shock... It happens when you find yourself in unfamiliar territory with no way out. Everything seems a little weird. The food tastes strange. The scenery is unsettling. The people dress differently, and you can't understand a word they say. You're in a foreign culture, and you go into shock! It feels like severe homesickness, with butterflies in the stomach, tight chest muscles, and that sense of panic that makes you want to run for your life. You can't think normally. My only thought was, *Beam me up, Scotty. I've got to get out of here—now!*

If the day had ended in Uliastai, I would have bounced back in no time. Unfortunately, the chaotic plane trip and the 30-minute ride across the prairie to tour Uliastai, snacking on mutton and yak milk, were only a foretaste of our longest day. What came next was the longest ride.

During our brief meal in Uliastai, the mayor surprised us with an announcement: "We have a special treat planned for you. We're taking you to the Mongolian Resort."

We looked at each other and shrugged. *There's nothing around here, so it must be outside of town.*

We crammed our group, luggage, the mayor, and drivers into two jeeps and headed across the prairie. You must understand, there were no roads. We're talking literally "across the prairie!" We dodged boulders, crossed riverbeds, swerved just in time to avoid sheer drop-offs, and bounced along… always bouncing… with a stiff breeze in our faces.

After two hours, the jeeps stopped beside a river, and I remembered what Hogan had told us at my house in Michigan: "You've got to go to Mongolia, guys. It's got the greatest fishing in the whole world! They've got these skinny fish so long that when you drape one over your shoulder, the head touches your toes in front and the tail touches your heels in back! You need heavy-duty ocean fishing line to reel them in."

We had brought our fishing poles with heavy-duty line just for this occasion. Hogan excitedly jumped out of the jeep. "Okay, guys, it's time to catch some of the big ones!"

We fished valiantly for an hour without a nibble. Once I thought I had caught something only to discover that my lure had snagged a rock. I pulled out my knife to free the line when our driver motioned: "No, no, no!" Just like that, he dove into the river, unhooked my lure, and brought it back to me, his hands dripping with icy mountain water. I smiled and dug into my backpack, handed him two chocolate bars, and we became fast friends.

Hogan eventually walked upriver and returned with a fourteen-inch fish that nobody could identify. We teased him and said, "Check it out! If you throw this one over your shoulder, how close does it come to your heels and toes?" At least we weren't totally skunked.

When Hogan decided we'd fished long enough, we jumped back into the jeeps for another jaunt across the floodplain. This time our ride felt like a compact roller coaster. It was like a giant had spread out his fingers across the land and we were riding up and over each knuckle.

Another wave of culture shock assaulted me. *What on earth are we doing out here? What if we hit a rock and break an axle? How would we ever get back? We'd have to walk for days. The mayor wants to show us a good time at the Mongolian Resort, but we don't need this!*

After five hours of the jerky roller-coaster ride across Mongolia, the mayor pointed to a spot of light on the mountainside. The resort was only a mile away. We had left Ulaanbaatar on a hot morning, spent a warm afternoon in Uliastai, and now we were shivering in the chilly mountain air of "Nowhere" with storm clouds looming overhead. At this point, we had been bouncing around on the prairie for five hours and I was exhausted, both physically and emotionally. All I could think was: *This resort had better be something spectacular!*

When the jeeps finally pulled to a stop, the mayor grinned and pointed. I couldn't believe my eyes. All I saw were two round tents next to a log shack that smelled like old mutton.

This was culture shock at its worst! Like I said, when you're in the middle of it, you can't think straight. My nerves were frazzled, and I was just plain angry. I jumped out of the jeep, stomped over to Hogan, grabbed him by the neck and said, "Hogan, this time you've gone too far!" My hands were still around his throat when Phil's voice boomed over my shoulder, "Hogan, I resign from the board of ELIC, effective now!" Hogan looked back and forth from me to Phil and let out a big hearty belly laugh. As soon as I heard his laughter, it felt as though someone pulled a cork out of my heel and the anger drained into the ground. The next thing I knew, I was laughing too. Once again, Hogan's humor had diffused the tension. Had he not done that, who knows what would have happened?

```
Date: July 5, 1992
Location: The Mongolian Resort
Event: A Day in a Ger
```

IF THIS ISN'T THE END OF THE EARTH…

I woke up much more cheerful after a good night's sleep. We were surrounded by the bright colors of a Mongolian "ger" (house) which is shaped like a round circus tent. It looked friendlier in the daylight. The walls were four feet high, and the roof slanted up to a large hole at the peak which was held up by brightly colored poles of red, blue, yellow, and green. The walls and tables sported the same bright colors with intricate inlaid designs.

The beds around the perimeter were built for small Mongolian people and my feet hung over the end so far that my toes nearly touched the head of the bed a foot away. They were odd little beds, and I remembered how strange it had felt last night when a young gal came in and tucked the blankets around each of us. I had felt like I was in a cocoon. It was a funny situation. We all started laughing.

This morning, our little chambermaid was busy lighting a fire in the potbelly stove that stood in the center of the ger, while another young girl brought bowls and spoons to the tables that encircled the stove. I asked for her name, and she said something long and confusing that had a "Ch" sound, so I nicknamed her "Church Mouse." She giggled every time we called her that.

Hot yak milk, dried yogurt pellets, and mutton soup were not my idea of an appetizing breakfast! The best part of the meal was the hot water, which I poured over instant oatmeal from my backpack and also used to make a hot Tang orange drink.

Once breakfast was over, we wondered what the mayor had in mind for the rest of the day. It didn't take long to figure out that Mayor Harloh's idea of entertaining Americans at the Mongolian Resort meant doing nothing. We listened to the raindrops sizzle when they hit the stove. We watched an old veteran of foreign wars nod off to sleep in his chair. Tom lost a 2-1 Chess championship with the mayor of Uliastai, while Phil, Patsy, and I taught the chambermaids to play Hearts. That was the extent of the action.

I kept wondering: *What are we doing here? Did we go through hell to get here just so we could sit around and play cards? How is this using my Labor?*

I had to think this through… We came to Uliastai to meet the mayor. He had invited ELIC to come to his village and determine the preparations required before sending teachers. Instead of showing us the situation in Uliastai, the mayor was "showing us a good time" at the Mongolian Resort. Was he trying to bump us off? If the trip didn't kill us, the mutton and goat-milk yogurt could finish the job. My father always used to say, "Man thinks but the Lord leads." Apparently, God had another purpose for this trip.

Then Hogan said something that made it easier to go with the flow. "Did you know that Jesus talked about us being at this very spot 2000 years ago?"

"What do you mean?"

He got a twinkle in his eyes. "The Bible says in the book of Acts:

'You will receive power when the Holy Spirit comes upon you; and you will be my witnesses in Jerusalem, and in all Judea and Samaria, and to the ends of the earth."

"Well, guys, if this isn't 'the end of the earth,' then you can definitely see it from here!"

```
Date: July 5, 1992
Location: The Mongolian Resort
Event:  Missing my evening soak
```

HOT TUB HEAVEN

Hogan had a backache and so did I!
The ride up the mountain had taken its toll.

The mayor had finally explained to us the reason this resort was so special. It had natural hot springs, and he suggested we go down for a soak in the tubs. He didn't have to ask twice before Hogan and I headed out to the bath house. Not only would it feel good on our backs, but it would give us something to do.

A little shack down the trail housed two old-fashioned porcelain tubs on legs. It was a clever set-up. A corked pipe poked through the wall and hung over the tub. When Hogan pulled the cork out of the pipe, the water gushed out. He discovered that a similar cork fit perfectly into the bottom of the tub. When the tub was full, we simply put the first cork back into the pipe while we soaked. When we pulled out the second plug, the water would drain out of the tub.

As the first tub began to fill, the water surprised me. It was very hot and very yellow. Hogan quickly jumped in and, while the second tub was filling, I decided to take a little walk outside to check out the source of the springs.

I followed the stream up a trail to where the water bubbled up out of the ground. On the way, I saw a flock of sheep warming their feet in the water between the spring and the bathhouse. One sheep felt the urge and just let nature take its course. These were truly "natural" hot springs. The earth heated the water, and the sheep added the color.

Back in the bathhouse, Hogan was soaking away and singing his heart out. He had no clue what I had just discovered and was happy as a clam. To him, it was "Hot Tub Heaven."

The moral of the story is: *Where you choose to focus your attention will determine your contentment level far more than the facts of the situation.* Hogan chose to focus on the heat instead of the color, and he was blissfully content!

Date: July 6, 1992
Location: The Mongolian Resort
Event: Major Bad News!

GOOD NEWS, BAD NEWS

I wonder why they're looking at us and laughing...

It was our second morning at the Mongolian Resort. Rain was still pouring through the hole in the roof, soaking all the shoes we had left around the fire to dry. Hogan and Bob sat across the room whispering. Then they looked at Tom and me and laughed.

Tom and I decided to whisper our own jokes and point back at them. Finally, Hogan jumped up and came over to us.

"Okay, guys. I have some good news and some bad news!"

"Yeah?"

"The good news is that after four days of travel, we've finally reached the ends of the earth. This is about as far out as you can go."

"Okay..."

"The bad news is that it looks like we're going to be here for a long time. The mayor just received news from Ulaanbatar that the government of Mongolia has run out of travel money.

They can't buy fuel for planes, so all domestic flights have been grounded. There's no way back to the capital." He shrugged his shoulders nonchalantly. *"We're stranded!"*

We stared at him, then Tom started laughing.

"That was a good one, Hogan. You had us going for a minute."

Hogan didn't laugh.

I said, "You are kidding, right? We have to get home. We've got work to do."

Hogan shook his head. "It's no joke."

Phil pulled out his "Emergency Evacuation" card, but there was no telephone at the resort, so we had no way to request an evacuation.

Tom said, "There must be *some* solution."

Hogan motioned for the mayor to join us, and he explained our only option. "If you want to travel by horseback, it's 40 days over the mountains to Ulaanbaatar, or about 30 days if you know the way."

We gawked at each other. *Who knew the way?*

I could see that the mayor felt deeply disturbed by the news. After all, he was responsible for inviting us. He said, "Let me go to work on this and see if I can come up with a plan."

Suddenly, this man was no longer the mayor of an obscure little town nobody cared about in the middle of nowhere—he was a significant government official with connections who held our future in his hands. That's when God began the work of changing my heart. Although I hadn't been crazy about the mayor's idea of hospitality, I found myself developing a soft spot in my heart for him. He was the only man who could save us from this predicament.

Isn't it amazing how God can do that? He is able to turn the most dreadful situation into an answer to our prayers.

Date: July 7, 1992
Location: The Mongolian Resort
Event: A Hearty Meal

THE MONGOLIAN BARBECUE

The pace was picking up!

We were heading back to Uliastai. The mayor needed to be in his city in order to work on a plan to extricate us from Central Mongolia and return us to the capital. But first, he insisted that we end our visit to the Mongolian Resort with a traditional banquet. We didn't especially care to stay, but Mongolian hospitality prevailed.

As a prelude to the banquet, the mayor led us outside to witness the killing of the fatted lamb. An official-looking man dressed in a black coat, tie, and top hat laid a clean white cloth over the grass. His assistant then brought him a newly shorn sheep, which he flipped onto its back as he gathered its hooves into one hand. When the sheep grew very still, he took out a surgical knife and cut a long slit in its chest. Then he quickly reached in and pulled out its heart. We could still see it pumping! The only sound we heard was a slight gasp from Patsy as the "doctor" squeezed off the blood flow to the heart and the sheep stopped breathing. I think I also stopped breathing as I watched.

The mayor then told us to wait inside while they cut up the meat. When it appeared, it looked like they had thrown away the good meat, leaving only the fatty parts. We figured that winters are so cold in Mongolia that they need to eat a lot of fat to stay warm.

The cook carried in a big metal milk jug, set it on the table, and carefully laid hot rocks in the bottom. Then he dropped hunks of meat down onto the rocks and poured in boiling water. When the water hit the rocks, it sizzled and made steam.

Finally, the meat was cooked, and we had our banquet. Steamed meat doesn't look too appetizing, but we were hungry.

Hogan said, "Okay, guys, let's dig in and show an incredible amount of enthusiasm for this meal." We hadn't been a bit excited about any of their food up to this point, but now we dug in with both hands and Tom said, "The mayor is going to be impressed. We're actually eating this!" The locals seemed very pleased. The mayor laughed and said, "Now you look Mongolian!"

We won the heart of the cook that day. He'd been raised under communism and taught to believe that all Americans were bad. The Soviets had lost their power only two years prior to our visit, and in that time, only one American had made his way to the Mongolian Resort. The cook had been astonished to discover that Americans could be so nice. Now that we were enjoying his food, he decided that he liked Americans, and we had a friendly conversation with him over steamed meat.

It seemed very fitting to end this strange visit to the Mongolian Resort with the "Feast of the Fatted Lamb." After three days of old mutton and yellow water, in my mind the mascot of The Mongolian Resort would forever be the sheep!

Date: July 7, 1992
Location: Uliastai Hotel
Event: A threat to our well-being

THIEVES, THUGS & BANDITS

There was no time for fishing on the return trip. Hogan threatened to troll for fish as we drove through creek beds that had been empty three days earlier but now ran knee-deep with rainwater. He was trying to distract us from the two questions looming in everyone's mind: *How would we get back to the capital? When would we ever get home?* It was a quiet journey across the prairie to Uliastai.

As soon as we arrived, the mayor went right to work on his plan—a scheme to swap fuel for a plane. He got on the two-way radio and talked to the governor who talked to MIAT. No one talked to us. Eventually he contacted a pilot who was stranded in another town and told him, "If you will come to Uliastai and pick up the Americans, I will give you enough fuel to reach the capital." The mayor felt so responsible for us that he was willing to sacrifice his own city's petroleum supply to get us home. I was truly grateful.

The pilot accepted the mayor's offer, but then we had another problem. The rain made it impossible to land a plane without instruments. We would have to wait for the rain to stop.

We checked into the Uliastai Hotel and couldn't help but notice a row of "thugs" sitting on the entrance wall and watching our every move. We deposited our luggage in our rooms and most of us left with the mayor to tour the town, while two of us stayed in the room with the luggage. Sure enough, the thieves broke in and were surprised by our "luggage guards." Their plan was foiled—at least for the moment.

In the wee hours of that night, the wannabe bandits got drunk and came banging on the windows. Tom and I felt pretty safe on the second floor, but Phil and Patsy were downstairs, and when the thugs banged on her window, Patsy went berserk. She cowered in a corner waiting to beat them with a stick if they dared to climb in through her window. That's where she spent the night.

When we saw Patsy in the morning, she looked like death warmed over. She said, "Phil, I will not spend another night in Uliastai!"

There was nowhere else to go.

Phil discussed the problem with the mayor, and we never heard how he handled the problem, but every one of those thieves, thugs, and bandits disappeared that day and were never seen again—at least not by us.

Date: July 8, 1992
Location: Uliastai
Event: The Tour

DON'T YOU LOVE IT WHEN A PLAN COMES TOGETHER!

Finally, we got to do what we came here to do!

Through all those frustrating days when we wondered what on earth we were accomplishing at the Mongolian Resort, Hogan would smile and say, "Don't you love it when a plan comes together?" Although he was being facetious, his humor always brightened our outlook, and his little phrase became the byword of our trip.

But today the plan was actually coming together. While we waited for the rain to stop, the mayor took us on an official tour of Uliastai, population 22,000. He walked us through the government building to his office where official negotiations with the teachers would be conducted. He took us to the university and showed us the classrooms where they would teach. Then he led us through the Soviet-style housing complex where the teachers would live. The gray building with dark hallways and uneven steps felt dismal and foreboding, yet the apartments themselves were decorated in bright colors and looked quite appealing.

That evening, the mayor took us to his own home for dinner and we were delighted to discover that his wife's Mongolian cuisine tasted much better than any we had experienced to date. We grew very fond of his family during that meal.

By the end of the day, Hogan was convinced that his teachers could indeed survive in Uliastai. The concept was turning into a plan and once these arrangements had been made, our trip no longer felt like a waste. It had been worth it after all.

I went to bed that night with a feeling of "Mission Accomplished." I love it when a plan comes together!

Date: July 9, 1992
Location: Uliastai Airport
Event: A Miracle Just in Time

WINDOW FROM HEAVEN

It had rained continuously for five amazingly long days. This was unheard of in the steppe region of Mongolia. We felt like Noah trapped on the ark. We had played all the cards and chess that we could play, and the mayor was ready to send us home. He got on the radio and contacted the airport officials in western Mongolia where our plane was waiting.

"The sky is clear. Send the plane."

But it was still raining! We loaded ourselves into the jeeps anyway and sloshed our way across the prairie to the meadow where we had landed five days earlier.

Before long we heard a plane approaching and a raindrop splattered on my glasses when I looked up toward the sky. We could hear it circling above the clouds, but apparently the pilot could not see the ground to land between the mountains. My heart sank as the sound slowly faded away. I thought: *That was our only ride back to the capital. Now we're truly stranded.*

Pretty soon we heard the plane again. We were all praying like crazy, and to our amazement, the clouds parted just enough for a plane to fly through! It appeared suddenly beneath the clouds, about 100 feet off the ground.

We laughed and cheered. Five days earlier, we had cringed at the thought of boarding a MIAT prop plane. Today, the old thing never looked so good. It flew in on a wing (the pilot's), a lie (the mayor's), and a prayer (ours). We quickly dubbed that little patch of blue sky our "window from heaven."

When the pilot came off the plane, he was madder than hops! He'd been tricked by the mayor who had told him the sky was clear, when in reality the clouds were so thick that he'd barely made it through, and now his plane was out of fuel. He would have crashed if not for that one small opening in the sky.

The pilot was in no mood to negotiate with the mayor and informed him in no uncertain terms that he had only four seats available. We watched anxiously as they carried on a lengthy discussion, and all at once Air Dan, our Mongolian translator, stalked away and went to the jeep to pout. Hogan took over negotiations with the pilot who spoke broken English.

"You have nine people. I have four seats. I take eight Americans, but Mongolian interpreter must stay!"

We understood why Air Dan had left in a huff. He lived in Ulaanbaatar and had no more desire to be stranded in Uliastai than the rest of us.

Hogan said to the pilot, "We came as a team, and we will leave as a team."

We gestured to him and said, "Maybe it's okay to let the interpreter stay. After all, he's Mongolian. He can find his way home, but we need to go!"

Hogan shook his head emphatically: "We're a team. We stick together!"

He finally bribed our way onto the plane—all nine of us! After days of scheming, our entire team was cleared to board, thanks to the hard work of Hogan, the mayor, the pilot, and a "window from heaven."

Date: July 9, 1992
Location: Uliastai Airport
Event: A Fond Farewell

FAREWELL TO THE MAYOR

I thought it would be easy to say goodbye to the mayor of Uliastai, but my heart had softened, and I actually choked up a bit when it was time to leave. These past three days I had watched him work his tail off pulling strings to get us onto this plane. We owed him big time!

The mayor thanked us for coming and assured Hogan that he wanted English teachers at the university. Then he looked at me and said, "Would you pray for me?"

I said, "Yes, I will pray for you!" It was a promise I was determined to keep. I put my arm on his shoulder and handed him my fishing pole as a token of friendship, which he received and held in the air for a photo. Later, I learned that most Mongolians are animists and believe the souls of their ancestors return in the animal kingdom. They won't eat fish, but he graciously kept the pole anyway.

As we shook hands in parting, I suddenly remembered my prayer at O'Hare Airport. Just one week earlier, I had absolutely no heart for these people. Now, after weathering a crisis with the mayor of Uliastai who had sacrificed so much on our behalf, I felt a close bond with him. In fact, I had fallen in love with the Mongolian people. God knew what it would take to answer my prayer. He wanted us to invest our hearts and resources into the work of ELIC in Mongolia, and He knew it would only happen if we spent intense time building a personal relationship with them. My love for the Mongolians came as a result of investing my Labor in spending time with the people and helping Hogan prepare for future teachers.

I realized as I walked to the plane that my attitude had changed drastically in the five days since we arrived at this grassy landing strip!

Date: July 9, 1992
Location: Uliastai Airport
Event: Reboarding the Plane

DON'T DO ANYTHING STUPID!

I had no choice. I HAD to do something stupid!

We had boarded the plane and were roaring down the airstrip when the pilot veered off to avoid a flock of sheep and the plane sank into the field. We unloaded and shoveled, and by the time the pilot had coaxed the plane back onto solid ground, 1½ hours had passed, and the sheep were long gone. The pilot pointed to the approaching thunderhead and warned that once it hit, the ground would be too wet to take off.

"It's now or never," he said. "Get on!"

We were running to the plane when I suddenly remembered Nancy's parting words, "Ben, while you're in Mongolia, just remember that you've got a wife and three kids at home. Don't do anything stupid!"

In that instant, it was as though time stood still. My thoughts flashed before me.

*We've just wasted 1½ hours' worth of fuel revving the engines.
The plane is overloaded. The runway is wet and slow.
We'll be taking off into a thunderstorm, in a plane with no
navigational instruments except a simple compass to fly
blindly between two deadly mountain peaks.*

Just then Tom nudged me and asked, "Do you see anything strange about those tires?" I checked them out closely as we approached the plane and counted four sets of bare cords showing through the rubber.

I thought: *What a revolting situation! How do I follow Nancy's advice? Getting on that plane is stupid!* But riding horseback over the mountains for 40 days eating old mutton is also stupid! If only Nancy could understand…

*It's not a matter of not doing something stupid.
It's a matter of choosing which stupid thing I'm about to do
is less stupid than the other stupid thing I'm about to do.*

Either option could kill me. Given the choices at hand and the limited time to decide, I said a quick prayer and ran for the plane. I figured: *If I'm gonna die, I might as well go fast.*

I boarded along with the others. The engines roared again, and we rumbled down the field for a long time on the soggy runway in that overloaded plane with bad tires. I felt a measure of relief when the wheels lifted off the ground. But then we were inside a thunderhead, bouncing up and down and around. No one spoke. I saw white knuckles everywhere as people on every side of me gripped their arm rests and waited for the worst.

After ten minutes of intense stress, we suddenly burst through the clouds right between two mountain peaks that seemed close enough to touch! I had to wonder if it was the incredible skill of the pilot or the guiding hand of God Himself that brought us safely into the sunshine. Either way, my grateful heart soared with that plane into the blue sky.

When we landed in Ulaanbaatar, we checked our watches and discovered, much to our surprise, that after all of the crazy finagling to get us back to the capital, we had arrived in Ulaanbaatar eighteen minutes ahead of our original schedule!

```
Special Agent: Tom
Date: July 10, 1992
Location: Ulaanbaatar, Mongolia
Event: Dinner
```

THE HEART OF A TEACHER

My name is Tom. I'm Ben's cousin and I have a different take on things. He loved the adventure of our trip, but what impressed me most were the hearts of the teachers.

When we arrived back at the capital, the teachers in Hogan's ministry took us out to dinner, and I was fascinated to hear what made them tick. It takes a unique breed of Americans to voluntarily subject themselves to the harsh conditions of Mongolia for an extended period of time.

One teacher who had been there all year said: "This is an important job and a wonderful opportunity. It's the first time I've ever felt like a pioneer, and I think I'm cut out for it."

Another shared, "I never dreamed that my own language—something I take completely for granted—could provide such an exciting opportunity of service for me!"

Ron Forseth agreed. "When you connect with the people face-to-face and one-on-one, it's wonderful! The Mongolian people have very warm hearts." We knew that was true.

Ron's family had arrived in March when the temperatures were still zero degrees Fahrenheit. They learned quickly that winter in Mongolia is brutal, and when his wife told us two couples had lost their first babies that year, Patsy's eyes welled up with tears. Then she said, "I believe that when the sacrifice of those teachers is laid to rest in the soil of their hearts, it will bring forth incredible fruit in the hearts of Mongolians."

The dozen one-year teachers had built a super-strong rapport through their shared suffering that year, and now twenty new teachers had joined them this summer. One of them, Doug Grey, was from Kansas City. He and his wife sat next to me at dinner, and they were extremely interested in the Uliastai region in Outer Mongolia.

"Tom, tell me about your experience. What did you guys think?"

"Doug, you're not going to hear this from Hogan, but I have to tell you the truth. I cannot recommend that you go to the town of Khovd (near Uliastai). The food is terrible. The climate is unforgiving. You can get stuck out there, and if you're sick, they have no medicine. In all good conscience, I cannot recommend sending you there."

Doug listened attentively to my report and when I finished, he said, "Tom, I appreciate what you're saying but I have to tell you, I think God has called us to Khovd. To me, obedience is more important than safety."

That was a powerful statement. Still, I said, "Doug, you don't understand. I've been to Outer Mongolia. I've tasted the food. We only stayed a few days, and it nearly killed us. You're going to be stuck out there for a whole summer! Maybe even longer if you get stranded."

He repeated, "Obedience is more important than safety. If God intends for us to die in Khovd, so be it. For me to live is Christ and to die is gain. But if He doesn't want us to die there, then He'll protect us."

There was nothing more to say. Little did I know how his words would haunt me.

The meal ended and Ben and I were in our room getting ready for bed when Hogan knocked at the door. "I just received a note from the summer team led by Doug Grey. I'd like you to read this."

I found my glasses and sat down on the bed next to the light to read the letter.

7-10-92

Mr. Hogan,

David reached into his bag, took out a small stone, and flung it at the enemy.

Your Khovd team is small, five people, poised, waiting to be sent to the giant.

Signed,
Judith Jacobson
Kurt Baillancourt
The Greys
Ken Stanley

Wow! As I went to bed that last night in Mongolia, I remembered our flight across the huge Gobi Desert and how I'd grown to love the rolling mountains and sparse population of Mongolia as compared to the cities of Tokyo and Beijing. To Ben and me, this was a short-lived adventure, but to these amazing teachers, it was a *calling*. I will never forget the incredible hearts of the teachers.

```
Special Agent: Ben
Date: July 11, 1992
Event: Journal Entries
```

A FEW PARTING THOUGHTS

On the long flight home, I had plenty of time to think through the events of our "journey to the ends of the earth," so I pulled out my journal and began to write.

> *"Now to Him who is ABLE to do IMMEASURABLY MORE than we can ask or imagine, to Him be glory forever and ever. Amen." —Ephesians 3:20*

ABLE: We prayed for safety—God opened up a Window from Heaven.

IMMEASURABLY: I'm continuing to pray for the mayor of Uliastai, and I can imagine meeting hundreds or thousands in heaven who were impacted by this small seed planted in the mayor's heart that led to an open door for English teachers to come and share the Gospel message.

MORE: I prayed for love in my heart — I fell in love with the Mongolian people through the difficulties we shared, especially the mayor, the Jeep driver, and "Church Mouse."

This assignment was truly an "Indiana Jones" kind of adventure!

```
Special Agent: Ben
Date: September 2000
Event: Latest Report
```

HOT OFF THE PRESS

As of our last conversation, Hogan told us there were fifteen new churches scattered throughout Uliastai!

After I came home from Mongolia in 1992 and shared my adventures with Nancy and our children, we began to pray every night for the mayor of Uliastai and his family. We prayed that he would come to know Jesus and through his influence, he would lead thousands to Christ over his lifetime. That has been our daily prayer ever since.

    We have also helped to send teachers to Mongolia, and those teachers have done a great job, not only in teaching English but also in sharing the love of Jesus. The mayor's son is now a Christian, attends a house church in Uliastai, and is sharing his faith with his father. God is answering our prayers for his family, and it's been a tremendous privilege to play a small part in this story that will last for eternity.

    We will continue to pray for the mayor, for his wife, and for Uliastai. I expect that one day in heaven, I will meet the mayor of Uliastai, his family, and hopefully many Mongolians who have come to know Jesus through his influence. The final chapter to this story is yet to be read on that final day.

ASSIGNMENT DEBRIEFED: LABOR!

What might your **Labor** look like if used for eternal purposes? Have you ever used your labor by partnering with a ministry?

Using your Labor can take many forms, such as building churches or schools, doing relief work after a catastrophe, or assisting in community development projects. No matter what form it takes, it always involves taking the time to go somewhere and give of yourself.

Tom and I had much to discuss when we returned from Mongolia.

We had used our Labor in the form of time, purposely setting aside our own business agendas to get involved in God's business in Mongolia. As we debriefed together, we realized that if we had said "No" to Hogan's invitation, we would have missed out on so many blessings. Not only did we experience the adventure of our lives getting stranded at the end of the earth, but we got to see God's faithfulness in new and wondrous ways.

Before I went to Mongolia, Hogan told me: "Once you get the soil of a foreign land in your sandals, you will never be the same." To this day, when I think of countries like China or Mongolia, those are no longer far away, distant lands to me. Instead, when I hear the word "Mongolia," I see the mayor of Uliastai and the faces in his family. Had we not taken the time to use our Labor in Mongolia, I never would have grown to love the people at the ends of the earth.

This was a new experience in "partnering" with a ministry. Our goal was to give encouragement to Hogan's team and learn what his ministry was doing in Mongolia. What we experienced was a two-way street of blessing. We discovered that when you team up with a ministry to use your Labor, you often receive more than you give! His staff gave us a new understanding of God's heart for Mongolia by allowing us to join their team, thus deepening our purpose for work at home. After we had built trust with them by observing their work firsthand, we were able to offer them fresh input from a business perspective. It was a give-and-take relationship from which we both benefited.

We came home with a wild sense of anticipation. Just think of all the Mongolians we may meet in heaven who came to know the Lord through Hogan's ministry! Tom and I felt very privileged to have been small pieces in that puzzle by using our Labor in Mongolia with Hogan.

Hogan described our partnering relationship so well in a letter he sent after we returned.

> "Have you ever heard the mountain climbing term 'on belay?' That's what the climber above calls out to his partner below when he has secured the rope. It means, 'Don't worry! I'm holding the line, ready to support your weight should you need me.' As Jan, Mark (Hogan's wife and son) and I get ready to move to China, the steep climb

ahead is a bit scary. But every time I feel insecure, I'm reminded that the Lord has given us good friends like you to hold the rope. So, hold on tight."

Our incredible journey with Hogan established a strong bond between our hearts and we were more than willing to hold his rope as he headed out on his next adventure.

Might God be prompting you to partner with a specific ministry by using your Labor, and in so doing, open your heart to a whole new world of people to love?

HOT OFF THE PRESS | 79

The Longest Ride

"If this isn't the end of the Earth,"
then you can see it from here.
Mayor Harloh, Tom

The Mongolian barbecue

Window from Heaven

Farewell to the Mayor

HOT OFF THE PRESS | 81

2ND ASSIGNMENT—
"I" is for Influence

Special Agent Ben's Assignment to Russia

Your assignment, should you choose to accept it, is to go to Moscow, Russia and use your INFLUENCE as a businessman to provide a platform for the Military Ministry of Russia to share God's love with the officers at the Nuclear Missile Base.

You will be one of a team of four businessmen who will share principles of how to succeed in business.

General Dick Abel will escort you and Colonel King Coffman will prepare the way.

★ Assignment to Russia

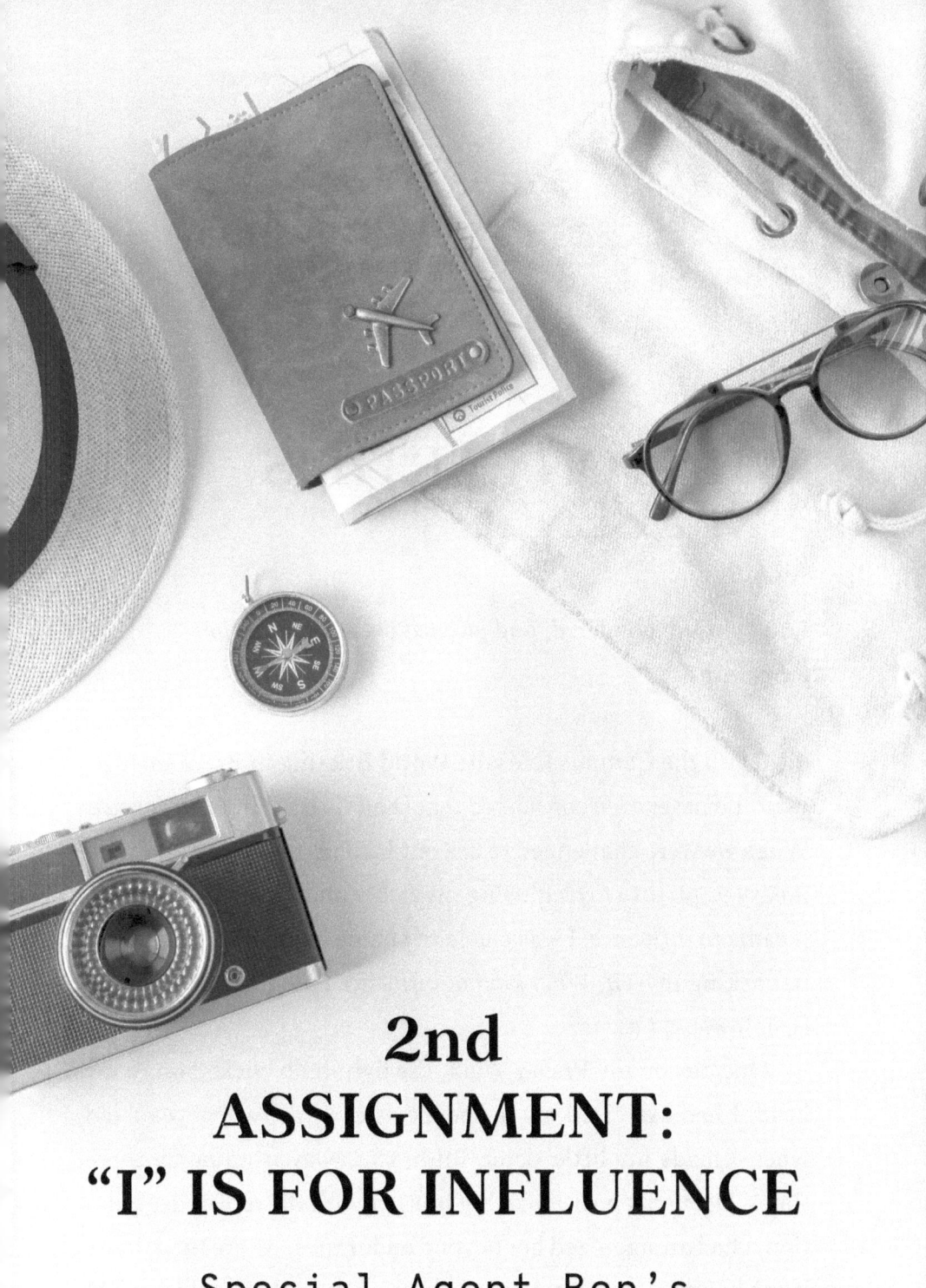

2nd ASSIGNMENT: "I" IS FOR INFLUENCE

Special Agent Ben's Assignment to Russia

Date: August 1997
Location: Petoskey, MI
Event: Prayer Walking

WHAT ON EARTH IS "INFLUENCE"?

I had prayed, pondered, and puzzled over that question for months!

Until the Campus Crusade World Briefing in Breckenridge, I'd never even considered that I had such a thing as *Influence*. When we were challenged to use our L.I.F.E. for eternity, I found it easy to picture myself using my *Labor* and *Finances*, yet when it came to *Influence*, I was clueless. I came home from that seminar asking myself, *What kind of influence do I have? Whatever it is, how would I use it?*

One day on my Prayer Walk, the light bulb clicked on in my head. I had exercised my influence as early as twelve years old when I made my little sister, Ruth, run away from home three times. Using my position of big brother with the tool of degradation, I had antagonized her beyond endurance. At the time, I saw it as a booming success. Looking back as an adult, I could see that I'd influenced Ruth in ways that were negative and destructive.

I still wasn't sure how to use my influence for good, but at least I knew I had some influence.

I began to pray each morning, "Lord, how do I use my influence in a way that will have a positive impact on people's lives for eternity?" The first month I asked God for a *heart to be available* for His use. When I figured I had a handle on that, I started praying for the *courage to be obedient* to do whatever He asked me to do. Because I was seeking with a sincere heart, I knew that one day God would show me the true power of positive influence. I had no way of guessing what might happen. I only believed that it would!

Date: October 1997
Location: Petoskey, MI
Event: A Telephone Conversation

THE GENERAL'S INVITATION

Why was I so surprised? I'd been praying about the idea of *Influence* for three months. Yet isn't that how it works? No matter how strongly we believe something will happen, it still comes as a shock when it does.

I had known General Abel for quite some time, so it was no surprise to hear from him. But when he called, his words were like hearing the voice of God.

"Ben, would you consider coming with me to Russia to speak at a businessmen's seminar for the officers at the Russian Nuclear Missile Base?"

My mind spun off in a thousand directions. *Me? Speak at a businessmen's seminar? To military officers? At the Russian Nuclear Missile Base?*

"Hello! Ben, are you there?" General Abel's voice came over the line, and I realized I hadn't said a word since he posed his question.

"Uh… yeah… I'm here."

General Abel went on to explain his request. "Ben, I realize I've caught you off guard. It must sound pretty strange my asking you as a businessman to speak to military personnel. As you know, I've been working with the Military Ministry of Russia, and Col. Coffman called the other day to present this idea for a seminar. Russia is downsizing their military and many of their brightest officers will need to transition from military life into a civilian career. He asked me to invite four American businessmen to explain to them how we do business."

My heart was pounding. This was big stuff! I might have waffled had I not spent three months asking God to change my heart. But this was the opportunity of a lifetime—the direct answer to my prayer.

"General Abel, I would consider it a great privilege to go with you to Russia! "

Date: Mid-January, 1998
Location: Moscow, Russia
Event: Morning Muster

A SPECIAL PARTY-MIX TEAM

It was shaping up to be a great team!

Our Fearless Leaders	**General Dick Abel**, retired Brigadier General. Executive Director of the Military Ministry of Campus Crusade for Christ. **Colonel King Coffman**, retired. An American living in Russia. National Director of the Russian Military Ministry.
The American Businessmen	**Ben Manthei**, owner of a concrete and construction business in northern Michigan. **Bill Dean**, Southern gentleman who owns a successful consulting firm. **Harry Jeffcoat**, owner of a Plumbing & Air Conditioning business in the hot and humid south. **Troy Bateson**, musician and trustee in a family construction company in Colorado.

A SPECIAL PARTY-MIX TEAM | 89

The American Ladies	**Ann Abel**, wife of General Abel, a most gracious lady who is never afraid of adventure. At ease in any culture, she makes people feel special. **Judy Manthei Schillinger**, my sister, four-time veteran to Russia, expert shopper. Came to lavish love on the Russian women and to encourage Col. Coffman's wife, Carrie. **Mandi Manthei**, niece, a newcomer, and eager participant in the women's activities.
The Russians	**Oleg**, a Russian military officer planning to retire. Soon-to-be National Director of the Russian Military Ministry. **Ludmila**, a retired Russian military officer. Assistant director of the Military Ministry Interviewer for Voice of Russia radio station. **Tatiana**, sergeant in the Russian military. Sang at the banquet, tour guide for the women's team.

Date: Mid-January, 1998
Location: Moscow, Russia
Event: Red Square Tour

TOURING THE KREMLIN

It was dusk in the city. Four of us had stayed behind to do a Prayer Walk around the Kremlin before going back to the hotel for dinner. My mind was filled with many thoughts as I pondered the events of the day...

Col. Coffman had started our tour of the city this morning by showing us the hotel lounge where he first met with officers before the Military Ministry built their new office. He introduced us to Oleg, who is a modern-day Saint Paul. Before Oleg met Jesus, his greatest passion in life was to kill Christians and Jews, and to train others in that pursuit. Today, Oleg greeted us like long-lost brothers.

Oleg took us deep into the heart of Moscow to Red Square. We entered through the main gate where he commandeered a Russian guide to show us *the largest cannon in the world...that never fired a shot*. The cannon ball itself measured four feet in diameter. Our guide explained that the cannon was useless because the barrel had been cast improperly. Ironically, the cannon points directly at the Kremlin where the Duma passes laws and conducts their business.

The next point of interest was *the largest bell…that never rang*. The creators of the bell made a huge form and filled it with molten iron, but the building caught fire while the bell was cooling and damaged the scaffolding that held the form. A five-foot-triangle fell out of the bell making it impossible to ring.

After explaining the stories of the cannon and the bell, the Russian guide shook her head sadly and said in a heavy accent rolling her 'r's, "Isn't it just like Rrrrussia? Nothing works in Rrrrussia."

We also toured a museum near the Kremlin wall which was filled with lavish displays of wealth from the former tsars. We were awed by the ornate clothing worn by the aristocracy. Even the harnesses for the horses were laden with gold and jewels. It was no wonder the starving people of Russia resented the opulent lifestyle of the tsars and supported the communist revolution.

That thought had lingered in my mind as we visited the mausoleum in Red Square. I know of only three mausoleums in existence honoring former Heads of State. I was surprised to realize that in my travels, I had now visited all three. The first was the mausoleum of Mao Tse Tung in Beijing, China. The second was the mausoleum of Ho Chi Min in Hanoi, Vietnam, where he is affectionately known as Uncle Ho. This visit to the mausoleum of Vladimir Lenin in Russia completed my trilogy of mausoleums.

Our visit to the mausoleum of Lenin was a very solemn event for me. It struck me that all three men overthrew their governments almost singlehandedly and established a new government with one common purpose in mind—to set up the perfect utopia. The common thread connecting all three was that each attempted to reach his goal by removing God from the culture. These men systematically destroyed churches and eliminated Christian leaders, believing they could create a perfect society based on man's superior strength and intellect.

Interestingly enough, in the half century since their regimes began, these three nations have created some of the most deprived cultures of the world. Decades after the fall of the Iron Curtain, many Russians are still struggling. The experiment of building a culture while denying the God who created life has doomed them to failure.

Three men lie in state in mausoleums that honor their bodies. Yet their deeds are recorded in the annals of infamy. From my perspective, they are among the most ruthless leaders in the history of mankind because they wiped out millions of their own people. Human life had no value to them. God, on the other hand, has given us a very high position on this planet. Each of us was designed by our Creator for a special purpose, and as we fulfill that purpose, our lives become rich and vital.

Throughout the day, I watched General Abel affirm people and help them to feel significant, regardless of his high-ranking position, much the same as Jesus did when He walked the earth. During our visit to the mausoleum, I was struck by the contrasting leadership styles of Jesus and Joseph Stalin. What an absolute lesson in the power of influence for good and for evil!

As Oleg, Col. Coffman, Mandi and I walked around the Kremlin, we prayed for the Russian people and especially for those in power in the Kremlin.

Little did we know that two weeks later Yeltsin would fire his entire ruling parliament! He reinstated many of them, but it was startling in light of our Prayer Walk.

Date: The next day
Location: Voice of Russia radio station
Event: A radio interview

CAN I ADD THIS TO MY RESUME?

I'd never been inside a radio station before. *What an interesting little stopover on our Moscow tour,* I thought. The station was called "Voice of Russia" and was the equivalent of our "Voice of America."

General Abel led us into the broadcasting room. A table laden with microphones was in the center of the studio. One of the padded walls had a large window which revealed an assortment of complicated recording instruments on the other side of the glass. A row of chairs lined the back wall. By now I was feeling intimidated, so I headed for the chair in the farthest corner. General Abel looked at me and asked, "What are you doing over there, Ben?"

"Oh, I'm just sitting where I can watch."

"Ben, you don't get it, do you? You're going to be interviewed."

"Uh… me?" I stammered.

He looked me in the eye and said with his booming voice of authority: "Front and center, now!"

I came timidly to the table. He motioned me to a chair in front of a microphone and Ludmila began her interview.

"Is this your first time to Russia, and what are your impressions?"

Three distinct impressions popped into mind, and I began to speak. "Yes, this is my first trip to Russia, and I have three impressions I would like to share. First…" I talked about the warmth of the people. "Second…" I spoke on the opportunities at hand. My mind went totally blank when I got to my third point.

Ludmila noticed my discomfort and quickly directed a question to the next speaker.

By the time we boarded the bus to leave, I had recovered from my embarrassment and was pumped up by the whole experience. I had never spoken on the radio before and here I was on "Voice of Russia" with my impressions being broadcast throughout the nation. I said to General Abel, "That was fantastic! I now have experience as an international radio speaker. Is this something I can add to my resume?"

General Abel shook his head. "Ben, you'd better learn to count to three before you put this one on your resume."

The line between humility and pride is often very fine.

```
Date: The next day
Location: Star City, outside Moscow
Event: Star City Tour
```

"STAR CITY" AND COSMONAUT VOLKOV

Have you ever imagined yourself inside NASA? On a personal tour? Having a private lunch with a real astronaut? That's the kind of thing you only see on TV… or when you're with General Abel. He gets us into the most amazing places.

Next, General Abel took us to "Star City," which is Russia's counterpart to NASA. This is where they train their Cosmonauts. My mind was on alert from the moment we passed through the first security gate. The facility surprised me. Although Star City housed their top space technology, the buildings were old with broken windows. No two steps were the same height, which kept us on our toes as we climbed from level to level.

I was fascinated by the Mir Space Station simulator. It was awesome to think that our own astronauts were walking around in the real Mir Station up in space at that very moment. Shortly before our visit, NASA had sent up a shuttle to dock with Mir but unfortunately it came in too fast, and the collision had damaged their station. Our guide took us to the simulator's site of the collision and explained exactly what happened, what broke, and what went wrong. It was exhilarating. Here we were, regular businessmen from America and we were privy to the secrets of NASA.

Afterward, they led us to a banquet room where they served lunch and introduced us to Cosmonaut Aleksandr Volkov. He had a deep gregarious laugh and spoke freely when we asked him about his days in space. When I asked about his family, he told us that he was born and raised in Ukraine, which seceded and became an independent nation when the former Soviet Union disbanded. Now he lives in Russia and his family lives in the Ukraine.

I couldn't help but ask: *"How has that affected your loyalties? Is your heart in Russia or in the Ukraine?"*

"I was thinking about that the last time I walked in space," he answered. "I looked down at Europe and the mountains near my homeland and then over at Russia. Do you know what I saw?"

I shook my head.

He said, "Looking down from space, there are no borders. Just one people!"

I raised my eyes heavenward and thought: *What a phenomenal lesson from a Russian cosmonaut!*

As I was looking up, I couldn't help but notice the ceiling. The whole room was paneled with rich wood. I had already told Cosmonaut Volkov about our veneer plant and explained the veneering process. Now I noticed that the ceiling was peppered with dents and stains.

I pointed up. "What happened?"

"Oh, this is the room where we celebrate our victories. We shake the champagne, and the cork shoots up, leaving its mark on the ceiling to remind us."

Cosmonaut Volkov then took us to the space museum. I guess I hadn't listened too well in school because I was surprised to learn that the first astronaut in space was not John Glenn, but the Russian cosmonaut Yuri Gagarin in a spaceship called Sputnik. When he returned to Russia, he became an instant hero. He traveled around the world and represented his nation to all the Heads of State.

Looking at Gagarin's picture, I thought about his instant fame and figured a lot of people must have envied his position. Yet, I realized this was a man who was born to be an astronaut and got to experience only a few brief moments in space before he was grounded. The Russian government could not risk losing their hero to a mishap. The same thing happened when John Glenn came home, until recently when he was finally allowed to return to space as a senior citizen.

As I contemplated the day at Star City, I asked myself: *Which would you find more satisfying? Soaring in the profession for which you trained your whole life, or staying on the ground because you're too famous to fly?* Who knows, maybe Cosmonaut Gagarin liked them both!

```
Date: The next day
Location: Nuclear Missile Base
Event: Businessmen's Seminar
```

SEMINAR AT THE NUCLEAR MISSILE BASE

We had finished our tours, and it was time to do what we came here to do. The seminar took place on the very military base where Russia's nuclear missiles were aimed at the Pentagon in Washington, DC. I looked around and saw nearly 50 military officers whose uniforms were decorated with stars and colorful medals. They watched General Abel lead our team to the table at the front of the room and sit in the center facing them while two of us joined him on either side.

He introduced himself as Dick Abel, Brigadier General of the United States Air Force, retired. After some opening pleasantries he introduced the rest of the team.

General Abel had given each of us our topics in advance with 15 minutes per talk. My subjects were "Integrity in the Workplace" and "How to Handle Difficult Decisions." I had no problem addressing "Integrity in the Workplace," but during my preparation time I had struggled with the second topic. In the brief moments allotted, how could I begin to address the difficult decisions one encounters in business, let alone the complex problems facing the Russian economy? Then I remembered where I go for answers to life's difficult decisions. That was it! That's what I wanted to share as a challenge point.

I told them that I go to a little book written by the king of a small country who was arguably the wisest man who ever lived on the face of the earth. His book is called Proverbs, and it has 31 chapters. On the seventh day of the month, I read Chapter 7. On the tenth day I read Chapter 10, and so forth. It is filled with wisdom that we can apply to our everyday lives. I challenged them to begin reading one chapter each day.

When I had finished my presentation, the officers asked me two probing questions:

1. "Do you really pay your taxes in America?"

    This question was heavy on the Russian mind because no one paid taxes if they could find a way around it. I told them that in America, we have a very good legal system and people pay their taxes or go to jail.

2. "We're curious about what you've shared regarding integrity in the workplace and where you go for wisdom. Is that the way all Americans think, or are you in the minority?"

    I told them that these principles were used by the founding fathers who drafted the constitution of the United States under which our nation had flourished. Yet our country is at a crossroads today for its very soul, every bit like Russia. A battle is raging for the hearts and minds of our people. The values we choose to apply as we move forward in the 21st century will determine the futures of both our nations.

A lively discussion followed. By the time we had finished, we had learned a great deal from one another.

```
Date: Later that night
Location: Nuclear Missile Base
Event: Dinner
```

PICKLED GARLIC CLOVES & VODKA

This was an honor to beat all honors. Here we were—four American businessmen and a General being hosted at a fancy restaurant by five of the highest-ranking officers from the Russian nuclear missile base.

We had the room to ourselves and sat at a long table filled with traditional Russian food. Each businessman was paired with an officer and a bottle of Vodka with two shot glasses. We had enough interpreters among us to keep the conversations flowing nicely. I noticed that things were a bit different at the other end of the table. Out of deference to Gen. Abel and Col. Kaufmann, who abstained from strong drink, the Russian general drank wine instead of Vodka and not very much at that.

Dinner was punctuated every five minutes with a toast, after which we were expected to join our hosts in chugging a shot of straight Vodka. We didn't want to offend them, but when we brought the Vodka to our lips, it burned like blazes! As you can imagine, by the end of the meal, the conversations were lively, and we formed friendships quickly. I'll never forget this meal where I learned the Russian custom of eating pickled garlic cloves and watched the reddening effect of Vodka chasers on the officers' faces.

When we finished eating, General Abel stood up and addressed the Russians. "Gentlemen, for the last 70 years we have been enemies. We have been trained, if need be, to kill one another. But now the Iron Curtain is gone, and we are here to tell you that we love you and Jesus loves you. Jesus loves you every bit as much and every bit the same as He loves us. There's no difference."

The General stopped to admire their uniforms.

"One day it won't matter how many stars are on our jackets. We're going to have to take off our coats and stand transparent before God. In that moment, only these questions will matter. Did we know Jesus and what did we do with Him? Did we embrace Him or push Him off to the side? Those are the important questions. But tonight, we are here to tell you that we love you and Jesus loves you!"

General Abel had brought medals from the Campus Crusade Military Ministry on which all five branches of the United States military were emblazoned: the Air Force, the Army, the Navy, the Marines, and the Coast Guard. He presented a medal to each, beginning with the lowest-ranking officer. One by one they accepted their gift and gave a short speech of appreciation. When their highest-ranking General finally came to the front, he said something that blew us away.

"I was born an atheist. My parents taught me to be an atheist, the military taught me to be an atheist, and I truly believed there was no God. I found my strength and meaning in life from my flak jacket, my Kalashnikov AK-47 rifle, and our nuclear weaponry, as well as from my own clear thinking and quick action. This is where I found my purpose and meaning in life. But when I would get alone and think, *Where will I live when I die?* I would feel extremely sad. Tonight, as a result of this seminar and my new-found friends from America, I am here to publicly declare for the first time—*God exists!*" He pumped his fist into the air and said, *"God bless America!"*

Our jaws dropped in unison. Here was a Russian General who had denied the existence of God and hated America. Yet his life had been so touched by what we had shared that he was asking God to bless America. On the one hand, it blew us away! On the other hand, isn't that exactly how it's supposed to be? When we're obedient to leave our comfortable homes and share what God is doing in our lives, then God is free to touch people's hearts. What a privilege! Truly, our obedience positioned us to see the mighty working of God.

```
Date: Even later that night
Location: The van
Event: Returning to the hotel
```

THE POWER OF INFLUENCE

My watch had all sorts of gadgets that were new to me, and I loved it.

I had lost my old watch and bought this one just before coming to Russia. On the way back to the hotel, I showed the guys in the van how I could push a little button for the light to come on and told them that was all I needed at night to find my way to the hotel bathroom. General Abel said, "Isn't that the way it really is? The darker it is, the less light you need to make an impact."

We debriefed about the dinner with the Russian General, and someone made a profound observation. When you travel to a nation where Christianity has been systematically stomped out for seventy years, you don't need to be a Billy Graham in order to have an impact. You only need to share what Christ has done in your own life and people are touched. They are hungry for hope and the love of Jesus.

As we discussed the concept of influence, it was amazing to contemplate. Whose thumb would you rather have on the nuclear missile button? An enemy who is bitter and vindictive toward you? Or one whose life has been touched by sharing God's love?

The power of influence, when used in a positive way, is truly dynamic!

```
Special Agent: Judy
Location: Tatiana's house, Moscow
Event: Ladies Luncheon
```

TO BLESS OR BE BLESSED: THAT IS THE QUESTION!

My name is Judy, and I am Ben's older sister.

"Why did Ben get to have all the excitement?" I wondered in envy. During our months of preparation for this trip, I had looked forward to enjoying a Russian adventure with Ben. But as it turned out, our teenage niece, Mandi, and I were not invited to participate in the same events as the men. I couldn't help but struggle in frustration when Ben would return each day from his outings to regale us with yet another exciting tale, while Mandi and I had simply visited with the women. Eventually I submitted myself to the fact that God had a unique plan for us, and I needed to embrace it wholeheartedly in order to be of service to Him and to those He would bring into my life. That's when I opened my heart to Tatiana.

Talk about the "hostess with the mostest"! I watched Tatiana ladle her fresh borsht into a traditional hand-painted bowl to be passed around the table and found myself amazed and humbled once again by the generosity of the Russian women. Many times, they went without eating that day, and possibly even the next, in order to serve a wonderful feast to their guests. Later, I learned that Tatiana had spent every spare ruble she possessed to extend this hospitality to us. As she handed me a bowl full of steaming soup, her smile clearly reflected the warmth in her heart.

I smiled back and remembered how my life had been touched during my first visit to Russia. I had come, not because I cared about the Russian people, but because I had been asked by a Christian seminar speaker to join his team and lead the prayer group. In the midst of my "duties," I had grown to love the down-to-earth, open-hearted people of Mother Russia. I had looked into their faces and seen a modest reserve that was surpassed only by their hunger for the words of Jesus. Whenever I handed them a Bible, they would point to my lips and say, "Tell me about Jesus with your mouth!" Having been deprived of spiritual truth for years, they had a terrific appetite for the things of God and wanted to know what Jesus was like in real life—in my life!

One elderly woman in the street had to beg for her daily food. When I handed her two dollar bills, she grabbed my hand and kissed it, and I was told that those two dollars would feed her for several weeks. I was so pleased to hear that on this trip, we would have the privilege of serving in a soup kitchen for the elderly, where they would receive their one meal for the day, and I hoped the lady in the street would learn about the soup kitchen.

Today, I looked into the eyes of these women and saw pain as I listened intently to their stories. The first woman wondered how long she should stay with a husband who drank constantly and slept with the landlady every other night. Another was exhausted from the constant search for food just to survive. The more I got to know these women around the table, the more I understood what made them tick. Three things kept them going—food, friends, and the love of Christ. Those who had not yet met Jesus lived out their days in hopeless despair. A third woman at our table told us her story, and as she spoke, another woman with sad eyes nodded knowingly. Like many Russian women, she had endured seven abortions and was dealing with nightmares of guilt from having killed her babies.

Oh, how my heart ached for these dear women! When we told them they would meet their babies in heaven, their faces lit up with joy. The sad one asked, "Do you mean I can say now that I have nine children instead of two?" I nodded and she was thrilled. It gave her hope for the future—for the love and joy that awaits her at the great reunion on the other side.

These women were survivors of the best kind. Although trials and suffering filled their daily lives, they smiled and loved life because Jesus loved them. They ministered to us every moment we were in their presence.

Have you ever journeyed to another country thinking you had something significant to share? Then, like us, you have probably experienced receiving more than you could ever give. It's quite humbling. We passed along a few words of encouragement while these ladies poured out their hearts and lives in a way we Americans seldom do. I came to Russia hoping to be a blessing and returned home as the one who'd been blessed!

```
Special Agent: Mandi
Date: The next day
Location: The Van
Event: Trip to the Airport
```

MANDI AND HER SPINNING WHEELS

My name is Mandi, and I am Ben's niece.

It just so happened that the sun was shining the day we left Moscow. Uncle Ben saw me gazing out the window and smiling, and he leaned over and tapped me on the arm. "Mandi, was I right?" I remembered immediately what Uncle Ben had said the evening we had arrived in Russia less than a week ago.

My first impression of Moscow was depressing! This was Aunt Judy's fourth trip to Russia, and she knew exactly what to expect. I had traveled through Vietnam the year before, so I wasn't totally shocked by what I was seeing. Yet, I felt the jolt once again of one's first day in a country with so much poverty and hopelessness. As I peered through grimy windows at buildings that looked gray and gloomy, the wheels in my head were spinning with thoughts of how incredibly blessed we are to live in America.

Uncle Ben had caught me off guard that night when he said, "Mandi, I know exactly what you're thinking!"

"Really? What am I thinking, Uncle Ben?"

He pointed out the window. "You're looking out there and wondering: *What on earth am I doing in this God-forsaken land?*"

"How did you know that?"

Chuckling, he said, "Because I'm thinking the same thing!"

Then Uncle Ben passed along a bit of wisdom he'd picked up from his previous travels. "Mandi, when we leave this place, Moscow will look entirely different to you. You're not going to notice the color of the buildings anymore. Instead, you will remember the hearts of the people and the friends you're leaving behind. You will think of Moscow in the fondest of terms by the time we leave."

Here we were a week later heading to the airport, and I had just breathed a quick prayer for Tatiana, Ludmela, and a student named Peter, when Uncle Ben asked, "Was I right?"

I couldn't help but grin. "Uncle Ben, you couldn't have been more right!"

It wasn't until four years later, as I reflected on this trip, that an even more profound realization struck me. Forty years earlier, when communism was spreading like wildfire throughout Asia and even into our own hemisphere as Castro claimed Cuba, my grandfather had purchased quite a stock of supplies and stored them away in preparation for a communist invasion that never occurred. Just prior to my own trip to Russia, my father and uncles had rediscovered Grandpa's stash and told us stories of growing up in fear of "the dreaded commies." Ironically, I ended up filling the extra spaces in my suitcase with socks from

Grandpa's stockpile to give away in Moscow. It finally struck me four years later that the very items Grandpa had purchased to protect us from our enemies had become provisions from God to "love our enemies" who had now become our friends.

Indeed, God works in mysterious ways, His wonders to perform!

ASSIGNMENT DEBRIEFED: INFLUENCE!

Recently, people strive to be an influencer on social media. But did you know that everyone who has contact with other people is already an influencer? Each of us has a unique "circle of influence" which is different from anyone else's. Have you ever considered how God might use your **INFLUENCE** in a positive way for eternity? Which people might be included in your "circle of influence?"

We learned some interesting facts about influence through this assignment. Did you know that 95 percent of people are reactionary, easily influenced by others, and simply reacting to people and events around them? Only five percent are proactive. Those are the influencers.

Once I embraced the L.I.F.E. principle, I decided that I wanted to become a proactive influencer and began to deliberately look for avenues to influence others in a way that would benefit their lives for eternity. I learned that there are three keys to becoming a proactive influence in the lives of others.

1. Set specific goals.
2. Make intentional decisions to facilitate those goals.
3. Dream big and be creative!

My first specific goal was to *ask* God during my Prayer Walks how He might use my influence to benefit others. My second step came when General Abel called about the speaking engagement in Russia, and I made an intentional decision to say, "Yes." But I missed the third step. I didn't dream nearly big enough. Fortunately, God did, and He used our influence to touch the General at the nuclear missile base.

During the tour of Moscow, I started thinking about what kind of influencer I wanted to be and what I didn't want to be. Being a person of influence does not mean having my name on a mausoleum somewhere. *Positive influence affects the souls of people in a beneficial way for all eternity.* I want to help my fellow man think through where they will live forever. I felt our influence had become truly significant when the general responded to our message.

People have asked why I travel around the world to help others when there's so much to do in the United States, and even in my own hometown. I tell them it's not a matter of choosing to help here or there. It's a matter of choosing to help *both* here and there—wherever God puts on your heart. That's what I learned from the Russian cosmonaut. The issue is not borders or nationalities or races or genders. The issue is people and their souls.

Are you touching lives in a positive way? Have you asked God to "expand your territory" (your circle of influence)? Are you dreaming big enough?

Prayer Walking Around the Kremlin
Ben & Mandi

The Largest Cannon
that Never Fired a Shot.
General Abel, Ben & Ann Abel

A Special Party Mix Team.
Ben, Oleg, and Judy at the Kremlin

The Largest Bell that Never Rang
The Team

Can I Add This to My Resume?

Colonel King Coffman & Russian Military Officer

3RD ASSIGNMENT—
"F" is for Finances

Special Agent Ben's Assignment to China

Your assignment, should you choose to accept it, is to go to China and use your finances to help the local ministries share the love of Jesus with the people of that land.

You will be escorted by Daniel, East Asia Director of "LIFE for Eternity" and his assistant, Peter.

You will need to trust God to lead you each step of the way through your guides.

Assignment to China

3rd ASSIGNMENT: "F" IS FOR FINANCES

Special Agent Ben's Assignment to China

Date: July 1997
Location: Colorado
Event: A Weekend with 'LIFE for Eternity' Ministry

A MAJOR CHALLENGE

We stood before a large world map in the hotel hallway and wondered where our next assignment might take us.

I began pointing: "We're already involved here in Mongolia, and over here in El Salvador. I'd like to see us help out here in China."

Mark, who was never one to make a hasty decision, said: "Let's see what the speakers have to say before we decide anything."

The others nodded, and we proceeded into the conference room.

This ministry had staff in nearly every nation of the world, and we were anxious to hear what was happening around the globe so we could determine where to next focus our attention. By now we were firmly committed to investing in the work of sharing God's love.

I was all ears as we received an update on the *"10-40 Window,"* the section of the world located between the 10th and 40th parallels above the equator. Of all the people who have never heard the good news of Jesus Christ, 90% live in this part of the world! The "10-40 window" was targeted for this conference.

The next speaker divided the map into tiny regions called Million Population Target Areas (MPTAs), which reflected the number of people represented in each section. A ministry director from each area updated us on the progress of their work and strategies for future expansion.

The next morning, I walked into the conference room with a spark of curiosity about what the day held in store. I'd been impressed by the quality and passion of the staff I had heard yesterday, and my heart was wide open to hear what today's speaker might have to share. Still, I wasn't prepared for what came next. The challenge definitely caught my attention.

"Would you consider adopting one or more Million Population Target Areas and make a four-year financial commitment of an amount greater than you could ever fulfill without God's direct supply?"

That was a radical concept—a **MAJOR** challenge!

An amount greater than I could ever fulfill without God's direct supply? Is it right to commit to something we're not sure we can fulfill? Can we expect God to intervene in our business affairs and bless us above and beyond our current status just because we choose to accept this challenge? Giving out of what we've already received is one thing, but making a commitment beyond our current resources is another. This kind of "faith pledge" would require a paradigm shift, a whole new outlook.

For years, I had seen our businesses as just a means of making money to pay bills, taxes, tithes, and take care of the family. Instead, it now meant looking at our businesses as a channel for

God to provide funds for *His* business. Like an electrical wire carries electricity from the power source to the intended appliance, so our businesses could carry resources from God to the specific places He wanted them to go. If He added to our current income, we would understand that He intended those funds to go toward a specific project.

This pledge would be a covenant of trust. We needed to trust God to provide, and He needed to trust us to forward the funds to where we had promised. We would be signing up to become part of something much bigger than we could ever accomplish under our own power. We may even discover a whole new purpose in life by entering into a covenant of mutual trust with the living God of the universe. It sent shivers down my spine.

The four of us had much to discuss after that meeting. The main thought going through my mind was: *We need a new business plan—an **eternal** business plan!*

Mark rubbed his hands together the way he does when he gets worked up. "It smacks of 'Name It & Claim It' to me! Just because someone promises to give a pink Cadillac, doesn't mean God is obligated to supply it. Can you imagine if we pledged a million dollars to build a church and they hired contractors based on our promise, and then we ended up not having the money? How would that affect our reputation? What about our integrity? I don't think it's wise to commit ourselves to something that's beyond our ability to fulfill."

Jim interrupted, "I see your point, Mark, but there's another way of looking at it. If we don't make a commitment in advance, then God might provide money down the road, and we might not recognize that He intended for it to go toward this project. Two or three years from now, we could forget all about this conference and end up using the money for whatever strikes our fancy. We could spend it on our own pleasure, which would give us a *temporary* blessing, instead of investing it into His kingdom, which would give us an *eternal* blessing along with deeper purpose and fulfillment."

I agreed with both of their opinions, yet these two points of view led to opposite conclusions. I looked at Tom, whose incredible gift of problem-solving had kept our team together through many disputes. He has an uncanny way of presenting solutions that incorporate conflicting points of view and create new options that all of us can support.

"Guys, I agree with all of you!" Tom held up his hand to click off the points on his fingers.

#1 Like Ben says, we need to develop an eternal business plan.

#2 Like Mark says, we don't want to be presumptuous and make commitments we cannot fulfill.

#3 Like Jim says, we don't want to walk away from here without making a commitment and forget this challenge.

#4 As for myself, I would like to accept the challenge."

Jim nodded while Mark fidgeted in his chair. Tom continued: "I have an idea. We could fill out a pledge card for whatever amount we feel led to give and add a qualification releasing us from liability if the money doesn't come in. That way they will know it's our earnest intention to support this area of the world as the Lord blesses us; yet they will also know they can't spend the money until it's in their hands."

As the four of us prayed about this challenge, our faith and vision increased so much that by the end of our discussion, we decided the four of us would adopt four MPTA's and support them over the next four years. The magnitude of this pledge, over and above all our existing commitments, went far beyond anything we had given in the past or could even imagine fulfilling in the present, which forced us to trust God to provide in the future.

That night, our pledge card became a solemn covenant between ourselves and our Master as we prayed: "Lord, if you bless us and as you bless us, we promise to recognize it as Your provision to meet this pledge." The next morning, we added a verbal disclaimer as we turned in our card. "As God provides, we will give."

Then we spoke with Daniel, the East Asian Director of Affairs, who also introduced us to Esther. We asked where they might need our help the most, and Daniel pointed to the Sichuan Province in the heart of China in the center of the 10-40 window. Could it be a coincidence that that was the same region where my finger had landed on our first day when I stood in front of the world map? I felt sure this was a confirmation from God. Our next assignment would take us to the Sichuan Province of China!

```
Date: Dec 28, 1998
Location: Sky Valley Park, CA
Event: Breakfast
```

A FAMILY TREASURE LOST FOR FIFTY YEARS

The Finnish pancakes tasted great. My family and I were enjoying a Christmas holiday in California, in the resort park where Aunt Lorraine and Uncle Al lived. They had invited us to breakfast, and we were catching up on each other's lives, when I mentioned that the guys and I were planning a trip to China. When Aunt Lorraine's face lit up, the pieces suddenly clicked in my mind.

"Aunt Lorraine, weren't you a missionary in China once upon a time?" I vaguely remembered her bringing us Chinese gifts when I was a wee little lad. Now I was hungry for details. "Where exactly did you serve?"

"I went to the Sichuan Province." A chill went up my spine and I thought: *Wouldn't it be just like God to lead us back to the very place where Aunt Lorraine had planted seeds fifty years ago?*

"What was it like, Aunt Lorraine? Tell us about it."

"Oh, Ben, that was so long ago..." Aunt Lorraine was now 74 years old with hair as white as snow. But I watched an amazing transformation as she leafed back through the pages of her memory. Her eyes began to dance.

"Back in 1948 it was very uncommon for a young lady to travel alone across the ocean to exotic foreign lands. That was quite an adventure for me! The first step was saying goodbye to my simple farming family and crossing the continent to San Francisco where I boarded a slow boat to China. Six weeks later, we reached the coast, and I boarded another boat headed up the Yangtze River. I had never slept with rats before!"

My wife, Nancy, cringed. "How could you stand it?"

Aunt Lorraine chuckled. "The American nurse sharing my cabin pulled out her bottle of Lysol and we soaked rags and stuffed them into every hole we could find. They never returned. When we reached Hankow, my journey came to an abrupt halt."

"Why was that?" I asked.

"This part is very important for you to understand, Ben. I arrived in China in the middle of the Cultural Revolution. Hankow was flooded with refugees fleeing the communist threat in the north. I had never seen such faces, haunted with fearful visions of death and destruction. All the boats heading upriver were packed with refugees and I had to wait six weeks before I could obtain passage on a boat. I couldn't speak Chinese, but I gained a strong impression of the severity of the Communist situation during my wait." We all nodded but none of us could truly understand. "When a spot finally opened up for me to travel again, I shared a tiny cabin with a Chinese couple who spoke no English, but they were very kind to me. The trip took seven days, and we passed through gorges where dozens of coolies on both riverbanks had to pull on long ropes to help the boat pass through the narrow spots."

Andy, my nine-year-old son, said, "That sounds like fun!"

Aunt Lorraine nodded. "It was! Then in Wan-Hsien, I saw my first familiar face in three months. Olive Gruen had visited our college, and God had used her to stir my heart and call me to China. There she stood waving her arms on the massive stairway up to the village. That night I had my first American food in weeks, and it never tasted so good. Believe me, Ben, you'll understand when you get there."

"Do you think I should stock my suitcase with granola bars?"

"That wouldn't be a bad idea."

My daughter, Lindsey, spoke up: "Did the communists ever take over Wan-Hsien? How long did you stay in China?"

"Well, those are excellent questions. I was barely there ten days when we heard a knock on the door and received a telegram from the American Consul General.

COMMUNIST SITUATION SERIOUS. PREPARE FOR EVACUATION.

"The Communists were heading our direction. I had just arrived and couldn't believe that the Lord would bring me this far just to have me turn around and leave immediately. We prayed long and hard that day asking God if it was His will for us to drop everything and run to safety. Instead, we decided to stay in Wan-Hsien until the communist threat came closer to our city.

We wanted to help the new Christians prepare for their eventual invasion by building up their faith so they could remain strong in the face of persecution. I celebrated the Christmas of 1948 with my new Chinese friends. All winter I studied Chinese and helped teach Sunday School. Although I could barely speak their language, the children loved the flannelgraph Bible stories! When spring arrived, we watched the country go bankrupt, which meant nobody had money. By summer, we could no longer travel to beautiful Kuling (now Guling) to escape the heat because that city had already fallen to communism.

When Olive got sick and needed to return to America, I had a difficult decision to make. Should I stay in Wan-Hsien without her? Would my presence help the Christians or cause them harm? My language skills were so limited that I decided to attend the Methodist Language School in Chengdu. That's where I had my last big adventure in China!"

My oldest son, Jake's eyes lit up. "Really? What happened?"

"As the Communists marched closer and closer to Chengdu, we prayed every day about our options. I always decided to stay. One night, I was suddenly jarred awake at midnight by someone banging on my door. 'Get up! Do you hear the gunfire? The communists are at the edge of town and a little German rescue plane just arrived to fly you out of the country. Grab your things and run!'"

"Wow," Linsdey said, "that sounds scary!"

"I didn't really have time to be afraid. We rushed to the airport, and I couldn't believe my eyes. The German pilots were loading a car onto the plane, and we had to wait while they actually took the doors off the car to fit it in! Isn't that crazy? With gunfire crackling in the distance?"

We chuckled. "That was my last memory of China. I lost all contact with my friends after the communist invasion in 1949, but I have prayed daily for them for fifty years. Come here. I'd like to show you something."

We followed her to the bedroom where an overstuffed chair sat in the corner facing a huge map of China. "This is where I pray."

I asked Aunt Lorraine to point out Wan-Hsien, and I was amazed at where her finger landed. "I will be very close to that just two months from now."

Aunt Lorraine's eyes lit up, and she pulled out a photo album with tattered edges. As she opened the pages, an idea struck me. "Could we take some pictures with us, Aunt Lorraine? Like this one of the Lutheran school and that one of the missionaries?"

"Sure. But I'll be very surprised if you find anybody I knew. Most of the Christians disappeared during the Cultural Revolution."

In my heart, I wanted desperately to find this little mission and bring back news to Aunt Lorraine of the Chinese Christians in Wan-Hsien. I held in my hand a lost family treasure and an exciting new purpose for my own journey to China!

```
Date: February 1999
Location: Beijing, China
Event: The Rendezvous
```

THE CHINA TEAM!

At the crack of dawn, Mark, Tom, and I drove to the airport in Traverse City, Michigan. Then we boarded our flight to Los Angeles for continuing service to Beijing, China.

Jim flew separately and met us in Beijing, along with the leaders of the ministry who would serve as our guides into China. Though we were weary from crossing America and the Pacific Ocean in a day, we greeted them with laughter and back-slapping as we waited at the airport to board yet another flight into Manchuria.

I LOOKED AROUND AT OUR TEAM AND THOUGHT:
This is going to be interesting. What a team of leaders!

Jim	Vice-President, Manthei Development Corp.
Mark	President, Manthei Development Corp.
Tom	President, Manthei Veneer Mill Inc.

Mike	Liaison between History's Handful members (us) and the national director of the country being visited (China)
Daniel	East Asia Director of Affairs, "LIFE for Eternity"
Peter	East Asia Director of Special Projects, "LIFE for Eternity"

We gathered up our belongings and headed to our next gate. We were finally beginning our ten-day adventure into the heart of China!

Date: February 1999
Location: Manchuria, China
Event: Arrival at Destination

ONE MISERABLE SINGAPOREAN!

Manchuria is frigid in February!

It was late when we landed at our destination city. Esther, a local pastor, and her assistant met us at the airport with two vans. We were bone tired as we loaded ourselves into Esther's van.

Suddenly Tom noticed that one of our group was missing. "Where is Peter?"

Daniel explained. "There weren't enough seats for all of us in this van, so he went in the other van with the luggage."

We settled back for the long ride to Esther's city. No one felt much like talking as we bounced over rough roads through the blackness of a Manchurian evening. We would have plenty of time to visit with Esther in the morning. Some hours later, we finally pulled to a stop in front of a hotel and dragged ourselves out of the van. A strange noise from behind caught my attention, and I turned around to see Peter's face. He looked like a whipped puppy and his teeth were chattering like crazy.

"Peter, what happened?" I asked.

"N-no heat in the v-v-van!" he stammered. Having come straight from Singapore where the temperature is a constant 90 degrees, his body was experiencing a shock. He shook his head and said, "Ben, you're looking at one miserable Singaporean!"

To add to his misery, the hotel was one bed short, so Peter had to sleep in the church, where they kept the thermostat set just warm enough to keep the toilet from freezing. He was cold on top of cold. Fully clothed, he crawled between two electric blankets and spent the night trying to thaw out!

Date: February 1999
Location: Manchuria, China
Event: A Midnight Fiasco

JET LAG & THE UPSIDE-DOWN CLOCK

There's nothing like that feeling of collapsing into bed after an exhausting day of travel and falling immediately into a deep sleep. That's exactly how I felt on our first night at the local inn in Manchuria.

You can imagine my shock when I was suddenly jolted awake by someone banging on our door. I cracked my eyes open to see that it was still dark and couldn't imagine who would pound so hard in the middle of the night. Soldiers with guns?

Tom crawled out of bed and stumbled toward the door. When he opened it, there stood Mark and Jim, fully dressed, their hair freshly wet from the shower.

Jim shouted, "Get up you guys. You're gonna be late!"

Tom sounded as groggy as I felt. "Jim, what are you doing?"

"It's 6:30! We're supposed to meet everyone for breakfast. We've got to go!"

I looked at my clock. "Jim, it's not 6:30. It's 12:00 midnight! We've only been sleeping for an hour!"

Jim marched to our window and pulled back the drapes. "Look at the horizon. The sun is coming up over that building." All I saw was the fluorescent glow of a streetlight.

Tom said, "Jim, you'll never convince me that it's 6:30! Now go back to bed."

Mark slapped his thigh. "I knew it! I knew I was right!!"

Out the door they went, arguing all the way down the hall. It was only in the morning light that Jim discovered he had put his watch on upside down.

Date: February 1999
Location: Manchuria, China
Event: A Week with Esther

ESTHER & THE MIRACLES

Esther was an attractive little fireball, full of spunk and vision. She was the pastor of a large, registered church in her city and had helped to add many church branches in her area as well. As she led us from place to place, we were fascinated to see the creative ways her ministry had contributed to their community.

The purpose of our journey into Manchuria was to help us catch the vision for how our dollars would be invested. Everyone who committed to investing in a particular MPTA was encouraged to travel with staff leaders into that region to see the work themselves. Daniel thought it best if we could see a mature program in China that would provide a working model of the ministry we would help to build in the Sichuan Province. Esther's ministry in Manchuria provided that model. We asked many questions as we toured and were impressed with her responses.

"We've heard that the communist government hasn't always been supportive of Christianity," I said. "How did your church become 'registered' and sanctioned by the government?"

"Oh, that's an interesting story…" Esther said.

It all began with a problem. Their small underground church had grown so fast that they could no longer contain it, so they went to God for a solution. It didn't take them long to realize that they needed to become "registered" and to arrive at a plan. They listed all the names of the top party officials in their town and began praying for them daily. They asked God for creative ideas of how to serve the leaders and the community, enabling them to become friends of the government instead of enemies. They looked carefully for needs in the community to see how they might be able to help.

Before long, people noticed that this group was doing good things for their town. But they still lacked one important element. They needed favor in the eyes of the local government.

One night, Esther heard a sharp rap at her door, and when she rushed to open it, what she saw made her heart skip a beat. Men in military uniforms with guns! "Come with us!"

They pushed her into a vehicle, and she felt sure that she was being taken to prison. When the car stopped, she was surprised to find herself at the home of a high-ranking military officer. The soldiers marched Esther into a room where she met a sick man. She was told that this general had been diagnosed with terminal cancer, given a month to live, and then sent home to die. However, his wife had heard rumors of a place where people had been miraculously healed, which had led them to Esther.

"You pray for the general!" they commanded.

Esther had never imagined anything like this and wondered if it was a trick. She shot up a quick arrow prayer to heaven: "Lord, if you want to help this man, I will do my part." Then she plunged in and prayed aloud for the general. To everyone's amazement, he improved immediately and then fully recovered from his cancer.

Of course, the general developed a soft spot in his heart for Esther, and he later used his influence to convince the local leaders to show favor toward her ministry.

"That's how the Lord answered our prayers to become a registered church," she told us.

"Wow, that's a great story!" someone said.

She then told us of another adventure which piqued my curiosity. Once they were "registered" by the government, they needed approval from a local official to buy land to build their church. One evening Esther attended a social function hosted by the mayor and seized the opportunity to ask him for permission to build a church. The mayor had not been supportive of the idea and was looking for a reason to say no. He happened to be holding an apple at the moment and suddenly had an idea he felt sure would guarantee her failure and give him a way out. "I'll make you a deal," he said tossing her an apple. "If you can break this apple in two with your bare hands, I'll give you permission to buy land and build a church." Esther had never broken an apple before, but she said a quick prayer, pushed in her thumbs, and twisted. Lo and behold, it worked! She shouted joyfully. "It broke in half! You said if I could break the apple, we could buy the land and build a church." She called him on his word in front of all his guests, and he was bound by honor to grant her permission. We marveled at the way God had faithfully led Esther and her ministry step by step. But personally, I wanted to know how she broke the apple!

"Ben," she said, "I'll show you how to break an apple under one condition. If you break it, you will help us add a new branch to our church." I took the apple, said a little prayer, and did exactly as she instructed. Sure enough, it broke in half. "Okay," she said, clapping her hands, "another branch has sprouted!"

In that moment we added the church in Manchuria to the overwhelming commitment we had already made to the Sichuan Province. We knew this would be an opportunity to see firsthand how God would work yet another miracle for Esther's church. By evening, I had learned a new skill, committed our group to help plant a new church, and formed a friendship with Esther. What a day!

```
Date: February 1999
Location: Sichuan Province
Event: Final Banquet Hosted by
       Government Officials
```

SEARCHING FOR LOST FAMILY TREASURE

We had traveled from Manchuria to Chendu in the heart of Sichuan Province and were invited to a banquet with the government leaders of the city.

Once you've experienced an authentic Chinese banquet, you've pretty much grasped the concept. This banquet was no exception. The highest-ranking official sat at the far side of the round table where he could face the door and see everything that happened in the room. Other officials were scattered among our group. The table was spread with the finest exotic food of their culture, which was nearly impossible for my American palate to appreciate. I quickly learned the art of cutting and moving things on my plate in order to give the appearance of enjoying my food, but eating it was a real challenge.

As he had done at every meal, Daniel pulled out the two photos from Aunt Lorraine and passed them around the table to see if any of the officials recognized them or could tell us how to find the little Lutheran Mission. I watched as each man shook his head to indicate that nothing was familiar to them. A few nights earlier at a similar banquet, one official had recognized something in the photos and told Daniel, "This is the town where I was born! These pictures were taken before my time, but I do know people there." He had told Daniel everything he could remember of his childhood town, and I had felt a small glimmer of hope. But it had faded into a dim memory, and tonight I was disappointed.

Have you ever felt called by God to do something in particular, and in the midst of it felt totally discouraged and ready to give up? I had experienced it once before in Mongolia and now it was happening again. I remembered how comfortable life was back home when I was doing nothing of eternal significance, and I just wanted to be in my own bed. I wondered what had ever possessed me to think I could accomplish anything by coming to China. I had tried my best to eat all the boiled snake, cooked dog, and fisheye soup that I could stomach and now culture shock threatened to overwhelm me. I began focusing on the negatives, and I didn't have to look beyond my plate. I decided then and there that this would be my last trip to China.

They say the night is always darkest just before the dawn. Little did I know that God was about to unveil a story before my very eyes that would encourage me until the day I die.

Date: February 1999
Location: A Hotel in Chengdu, China
Event: A Planning Session

A POWERFUL PRAYER

"How would you like to go to Wan-Hsien tomorrow and see what we find?"

We had just returned to the hotel to debrief and plan our next day. Daniel informed us that our tour of Sichuan Province was complete, and we had another day before we needed to return to Beijing, where we would part ways and fly to our respective homes. He wondered if we would like to use the extra time to track down the mission where Aunt Lorraine had worked.

Go to Wan-Hsien? Of course I wanted to go! I had given up on the idea and was thrilled that it was coming back to life. The other guys agreed that it sounded like an exciting plan.

"Okay," Daniel said, "we'll have to leave bright and early to see if there are any flights to Wan-Hsien."

We gathered around the bed, got down on our knees, and prayed that God would go before us to prepare a *divine appointment* for us when we reached Wan-Hsien. As far as I knew we had no contacts in that town and needed God to lead us to a person who could show us the way to the mission if it still existed.

A POWERFUL PRAYER | 143

PLATE XXII—A Bridge at Wan-Hsien.

PUBLIC DOMAIN IMAGE: Plate XXII A Bridge at Wan-Hsien, photogravure from a black-and-white photograph, before 1926, on a page from Donald Mennie's book, The Grandeur of the Gorges, Published 1926.

```
Date: February 1999
Location: Chengdu Airport
Event: Journey to Wan-Hsien
```

THE LIVER-SHAKER RIDE

We were up and running before the sun even thought about rising. If there was a flight to Wan-Hsien that day, we didn't want to miss it!

The man at the ticket counter looked puzzled when Daniel named our destination. "Wan-Hsien?" Although they spoke Chinese, we recognized the name and wondered why his voice had sounded so strange. After a lengthy conversation, Daniel bought the tickets and presented them to us with a smile.

When we questioned Daniel about his transaction, his story surprised us. "The man at the ticket counter asked for our destination, and when I said Wan-Hsien, he didn't know what to do. He kept saying, 'You want to go to Wan-Hsien? But there's nothing there! Wan-Hsien is only a little airport which services some cities up in the mountains. There's no hotel. No restaurants. Tourists do not stop in Wan-Hsien.' I tried to describe to him the city where your aunt had lived and when I mentioned the Yangtze River and all those steps, he finally understood. 'Ah so, you want *Wanzhou City*!' Apparently, the name of the town has changed during the last fifty years."

He handed us our tickets. "There's one flight to Wan-Hsien airport, and it leaves in one hour. Our timing is perfect. From there, we will take a bus over the mountain to Wanzhou City."

As we crossed the pavement for boarding, we saw that the plane was another vintage 1950 with bald tires. It was too late to balk. The tickets were purchased, and it was time to board. After a bumpy take-off, the 1½-hour flight was routine. The next leg of our journey, however, would make up for it.

Like the plane, the bus we boarded was old and rickety. We headed out of town, and as we began our ascent up the mountain, I wondered how the bus stayed in one piece. It rattled and groaned around the bumpy twists and turns. When we gained sufficient elevation, I leaned close to the window to look down, and my stomach flipped. There were no guardrails—just a sheer drop to a gorge several hundred feet below. I watched closely as we bounced around the next curve and noted that our front tire came within a foot of the edge. On another curve, I saw the remains of a crashed jeep at the bottom of the cliff. Several curves later, a bus like ours had met its demise. All this time, my insides were jostling about and struggling to remain intact.

Finally, we crested the mountain and began our descent. If the trip up the mountain made me nervous, the trip down was terrifying. Each time our driver pressed the brake pedal before taking a curve, the bus shimmied like a flopping fish. I suddenly knew why the other bus and jeep had crashed. Faulty brakes meant sure death on this mountain.

I started thinking: *Last night, sitting in the comfortable hotel, this trip had seemed like a great idea. If only I had known!*

I looked over at Peter. His eyes were closed but I knew his wheels were spinning. "Peter, what are you thinking?"

"I'm thinking..." he paused, then decided to go ahead and say it. "I'm thinking... *What has Daniel got us into now???*"

He couldn't have said it better. We knew that, for every mile we endured that day, we could look forward to retracing our tracks the next day.

But if the ride was a shock to our system, the next curve provided our first glimpse of what Aunt Lorraine called Wan-Hsien, and it hit me like a lightning bolt! Wanzhou City sprawled far up the mountains on both sides of the Yangtze River! It was no longer a sleepy town of 10,000 people but a major metropolis that had exploded to well over a million!

This is crazy! I said to myself. *Here we are in a city of over a million people sprawling up the mountain sides. They don't even speak English! Where do we begin to look for the little Lutheran Mission where Aunt Lorraine worked? It would be like trying to find a needle in a haystack, only the needle was lost fifty years ago!!*

```
Date: February 1999
Location: Hotel in Wanzhou City
Event: Arrival in Wanzhou City
```

A DIVINE APPOINTMENT

The bus driver had suggested that we stay at the largest hotel in town. "That's where all the foreigners go."

We had no idea what our next step would be, but a wise man once said: "When you don't know what to do, do what you know." We knew that we needed a place to sleep, to stow our luggage, and to catch a bite to eat. That was our only plan. We had no clue that God had been working through others behind the scenes to schedule a divine appointment.

Our taxi pulled up in front of a two-star hotel. We stepped out of the van and immediately a young Chinese woman rushed out of the hotel and hurried over to us. "I'm so glad you're finally here. I've been waiting for you!"

We were dumbfounded. "Waiting for us? We made no arrangements. How could you be waiting for us?"

Her explanation was simple. "Three days ago, you met the governor of Sichuan Province, and he asked us to watch for you. He said, "They might be coming to your town, and I'd like you to show them around. You'll recognize them. They're tall and they're American."

Our "hostess" worked for the Department of Religious Affairs and was an official liaison between the government and the church. We chatted with her over lunch, showed her our two pictures, and explained what we were trying to find. She said, "I'm way too young to recognize any of this, but I know a man who might be able to help. He pastors a registered church and he's over eighty years old. I could take you to meet him and see what he might remember."

She drove us to a large church where we met Rev. Zhang. When we showed him the pictures, his eyes lit up in amazement.

"This is the mission that led me to the Lord over fifty years ago! Unfortunately, many of these children were either killed or dispersed throughout China during the Cultural Revolution. As far as I know, I am the only remaining person in Wanzhou City who was part of this mission."

Unbelievably, within two hours of arriving in a city of over a million people, we had been led to the sole survivor of the little Lutheran Mission. Talk about a divine appointment!

```
Date: February 1999
Location: Wanzhou City
Event: Touring Wanzhou City
```

FOUND: A LOST FAMILY TREASURE

My hopes were dashed. Her name was not Miss White!

I had just pointed to Aunt Lorraine in the picture of the missionaries, and Rev. Zhang had said, "Ah, Miss White!" I thought, *He must have her confused with someone else and never really knew Aunt Lorraine after all.* I said slowly and politely, "My aunt's name was Lorraine *Beyling*. Miss *White* must have been someone else."

He smiled. "In Chinese, 'beh' means 'white,' so we called her 'Miss White.' She helped Miss Green teach young children while I studied at the seminary with Rev. Ziegler." His story matched Aunt Lorraine's perfectly, and we were amazed all over again.

When we asked Rev. Zhang if his church was still Lutheran, he explained that all "registered" churches in China are known as '3-Self' churches: Self-led, Self-supported, and Self-propagated. They no longer have denominations like Lutheran and Methodist. We also learned that our hostess was one of Rev. Zhang's three assistants.

Rev. Zhang and our hostess took us on a tour of the city, and

Rev. Zhang pointed out places that had been significant to Aunt Lorraine. "This is where Miss White arrived by boat and climbed up many steps." Then he took us up the winding mountain road where she had been carried by coolies to show us where the mission had once stood. He explained that both the mission and the school had been torn down some years earlier and replaced with apartment buildings. "The school was taken over by the communists during the Cultural Revolution, and when they outgrew their building, they rebuilt in a new location."

They drove us to the new school, which was in session, and said, "We will go inside."

The school happened to be celebrating their fiftieth anniversary as a communist institution. When Rev. Zhang explained to the leaders that our aunt had worked in the school prior to that, they received us with delight and were eager to learn the part of their history that had been lost to them. The principal brought out a large book for us to sign. Inside I wrote *"On behalf of Miss White, who helped in the school as a missionary in 1949 and is still praying that you will come to know Jesus as she has."*

On the way back to the church, we reflected on the honor our family had just received to represent the heart of God and be at the little Lutheran Mission at this special time in the history of the school. We sang a hymn of praise to celebrate.

When we finished singing, Rev. Zhang said, "I will sing a song that they taught me at the mission fifty years ago. Only song I sing in English." Although his voice was that of an eighty-year-old man, the words were ageless:

"Jesus loves me, this I know
For the Bible tells me so
Little ones to Him belong,
They are weak but He is strong…"

While he sang, it was confirmed in my heart that although our cultures had separated us as enemies for fifty years, we were truly brothers in the Lord.

When we arrived back at the church, Rev. Zhang introduced us to his other two assistants, one of whom we later nicknamed, "Cindrel." When Rev. Zhang showed Cindrel the picture of Aunt Lorraine, she said, "Ah, Miss White! I didn't know her personally, of course. This was before my time. But it is as if I knew her." Cindrel then explained that an older friend of hers who had died two years earlier had spoken continuously about Miss White. Even on her deathbed, she was wondering if Miss White would return to China one day. "Could Miss White come?" Cindrel asked. I shrugged. I couldn't answer for Aunt Lorraine.

As I spoke with that young woman, a Bible verse came to mind:

> *"Let us not lose heart in doing good,
> for in due time you will reap if you do not
> grow weary" (Galatians 6:9).*

I remembered Aunt Lorraine saying that she had prayed fifty years for the people of China, never knowing what it accomplished. Rev. Zhang told us that when Aunt Lorraine arrived in

1949, he estimated 30-50 native Christians lived in Wan-Hsien. At the end of the Cultural Revolution in the 1980s, he figured that number had grown to eighty. Today, the registered church has over 2500 baptized believers with approximately 15,000 in the underground church.

As I went to bed that night, I marveled at all God had shown us that day. Just twenty-four hours earlier, I was at my lowest point in the trip. Now, my heart was soaring.

Truly, man thinks and the Lord leads! He had led our family to commit ourselves to help in Sichuan Province, the same area He had called our aunt to fifty years earlier. He had led us to the exact spot where she had worked, in order to show us the results of the tiny seeds she had helped to plant. And what fruit we saw! Of course, the Lutheran Mission was only part of a larger team that God had used, but it played a significant role in sharing Christ with Rev. Zhang, who now pastors a large, registered church. Unbeknown to her, Aunt Lorraine had impacted the life of a girl who grew into a woman who influenced many others. Then, to hear of the exponential growth in the church these past twenty years was astonishing. Truly, the results of Aunt Lorraine's fifty years of faithful prayers will not be fully known until we reach heaven.

As I pondered the day, I believed God had given us a very special confirmation that we were indeed on the right track in using our L.I.F.E. to join His team around the world. I saw that each of our lives is like a single thread in a vast tapestry. Although we cannot tell yet what the picture will look like, when we reach heaven, our hearts will be thrilled to see how God wove our own little thread of experience with those of so many others to form an exquisite portrait of the true Church.

```
Date: February 1999
Location: Ben's house
Event: Telephone call
```

HOW TO BLOW AWAY AN AUNT

I couldn't wait to tell Aunt Lorraine how her prayers had been answered. I knew it would blow her away. I had already called her once on a cell phone when we first arrived at the hotel in Wanzhou City. "Aunt Lorraine, you're not going to believe this, but I'm sitting in the town you knew as Wan-Hsien, which is now called Wanzhou City. We just met a lady who says she knows an 80-year-old pastor. We're getting ready to meet him and see what we can find."

Aunt Lorraine had anxiously awaited a call back, but we couldn't get through to her the rest of that day, and we had to begin traveling early the next morning. Now I was home and had plenty of time to share our discoveries with her. I especially wanted to tell her about Cindrel.

"Aunt Lorraine, when we pulled out the pictures to show Cindrel, she said, 'I'm much too young to recognize her, but is this Miss White?'" Aunt Lorraine gasped. "How did she know me?" I explained. "You led a girl to the Lord while you were in

China and, for the last fifty years, that woman has talked about 'Miss White.' She said you changed the direction of her life. Even on her deathbed two years ago, she was hoping to see you one more time and thank you for sharing Jesus with her."

"That's amazing!" Aunt Lorraine sighed. "I didn't think I had done anything significant in my short time there. I had forgotten about that girl."

"Aunt Lorraine, when I told Cindrel that you had continued to pray for them these fifty years, Cindrel grabbed my arm and begged, 'Could Miss White p-l-e-a-s-e come back? There's so much we can learn yet from Miss White!' "

"What do you think, Aunt Lorraine? Would you like to go back and see how God has answered your prayers? Cindrel asked us at least six times if you could come. I would be happy to take you." I suddenly remembered my weak moment when I vowed to myself that I would never return. I might have to eat those words.

"Oh my, Ben…" Aunt Lorraine said. "I don't know. I'm almost seventy-five years old and that's a long trip. I just don't know, but I *will* begin to pray about it."

3RD ASSIGNMENT— Continued

Special Agent Ben's Return to China

Your mission should you choose to accept it, is to take your Aunt Lorraine back into China and reunite her with Rev. Zhang and the work in Wanzhou City.

You will lead a team spanning three generations so that I can demonstrate my faithfulness to all generations.

Peter will join you in Hong Kong as your translator and guide.

```
Special Agent: Ruth
Date: Summer 1999
Location: Mom's house
Event: Preparatory meeting
```

THE RAG-TAG TEAM

I'm Ben's little sister, Ruth.

What started as a simple phone call had mushroomed into much more. Ben was so excited when he came home from China that he just had to share his Wan-Hsien story at every family gathering. Of course, I egged him on because the story was truly remarkable.

When Ben called Aunt Lorraine to pass along Cindrel's invitation, none of us expected her to go. But two important things happened after she prayed. First, she received a formal invitation to speak at the 50-Year Jubilee Celebration in Hong Kong, where she had worked with Chinese refugees for ten years after her harrowing escape from China. Second, she received a formal invitation from the school in Wanzhou City to help them celebrate their anniversary as well.

Three months after their initial conversation, Aunt Lorraine called Ben to say, "I'd like to accept these invitations if you're still willing to take me, but I don't want to be the only white-haired lady over seventy-five years old on the trip. I'd like you to ask my sister, Cora to come along." The next thing I knew, not only were Ben and Aunt Lorraine going back to China, but also our mom, Cora, and Ben's son, Jacob. Three generations!

Ben went to China in the winter of '98, Aunt Lorraine called in the spring of '99, and now it was summer as we gathered around Mom's supper table for our first preparatory meeting of the "Return to China" trip in the fall. What an interesting group! Our 77-year-old mother looked like a twin to her sister, and we could easily imagine Aunt Lorraine joining us in prayer from California! They represented the 1st generation. Four of us represented the 2nd generation—Ben, Nancy, Judy, and I. Ben sat across the table and talked in excited tones about his upcoming adventure. I joined Ben's wife, Nancy, and our sister, Judy, as partners who would stay home and pray. Ben's sixteen-year-old son, Jacob, represented the 3rd generation. Ben would be leading a very unusual team on this trip.

"Whatever does a rag-tag team like this expect to accomplish in China?" somebody asked. We looked at the faces around the table and burst into laughter. What a crew! Two white-haired grandmothers, a high school kid, a small-town businessman, and some middle-aged women who agreed to pray. From that point on, we called ourselves the Rag-Tag Team! Ben reminded us that Peter planned to join the team at the Hong Kong airport and serve as the interpreter and guide on the trip into China.

After dinner, Ben led us out onto Mom's deck overlooking Lake Michigan. He read a Bible verse, and we assembled a list of concerns for prayer. By the end of the evening a sense of excitement permeated the group, and I felt privileged to be part of the team as a prayer partner. I had traveled on mission trips in the past, even served a year in Peru, and toyed with the idea of joining the family on this outing, yet I knew it was important to have a strong base of prayer support on the home front when traveling abroad.

During Ben's first trip to China, I dreamt one night that he and our brothers were murdered. I woke up sobbing. Immediately I began to pray for them and continued to pray over the remaining days of their journey. When they came home, I pulled Ben aside to ask if he had ever been in danger. A strange look flashed across his face. "Why do you ask?" When I told him about the dream, he quietly told me a story he had omitted during our large family gathering.

On the way home from China, Ben, Mark and Tom had decided to stop over in Israel for a brief tour. They had rented a jeep and driver, and they were winding down a ravine between Jerusalem and Jericho when they rounded a bend and suddenly found themselves in the midst of Arab men pointing guns at them. Being the open-hearted American that Ben is, he figured the men must be bird hunting and thought nothing of it when they quickly lowered their guns and waved the jeep on! It wasn't until the driver calmed down enough to speak that Ben learned the terrible truth. Those men were bandits, and the Israeli informed them that it was truly a miracle they had not been robbed or even killed. He had no idea why these men had lowered their guns.

I believe my dream was a warning from God and that my daily prayers somehow protected them during their time of crisis. Now that our mother was joining Ben on his next adventure, you'd better believe I was going to pray!

Special Agent: Cora Manthei
Date: October 28, 1999
Location: Hong Kong
Event: Golden Jubilee Week

A WHITE-HAIRED GRANDMA GOES TO HONG KONG

I'm Ben's mother, Cora, and I was not looking forward to this trip!

As the Rag-Tag Team came to my house each week for our preparatory meetings, my daily prayer was the same: "Lord, please change my attitude."

China was the last place in the world I ever wanted to visit. I had always admired my sister, Lorraine, for her work there as a missionary, and I had supported missions to China for many years. But the older you get, the more you like to stay in your comfort zone. Mine was right here in the USA, at my summer home in Petoskey, Michigan, and winter home in California. I had told Lorraine that I would consider going along to China, but I continued to push the idea to the back of my mind. One day I told my son, Mark, about the China invitation and Mark said,

"Mom, of course you will go! You'll enjoy traveling with Ben."

I suddenly knew I was going to China. And that was also the beginning of my sleepless nights. I would turn seventy-seven just before we left, which seemed way too old to be setting out on an adventure like this, with strange food and strange beds. What if I got sick? We prayed for these concerns during our meetings, but I continued to lay awake at night wondering what might happen.

I flew to California a week before the others so my body could get a 3-hour head start on jet lag adjustment. Misery loves company, and I was tickled to discover that Lorraine was dreading the food in China as much as I was.

On a beautiful day just before we left, I took a walk up the street to enjoy the California sun in our mobile home park and stopped to chat with a neighbor about my upcoming trip. The sky was so blue and as I looked up, I saw a cloud formation like angel wings on the back of a huge angel. I believed God was giving me a visible sign that everything was going to be fine, and a deep peace settled into my heart.

I left my worries behind and flew to Hong Kong. True to their promise, my sons saw to it that Lorraine and I would not have to "rough it." Our accommodations were superb.

The Lutheran Church of Hong Kong was hosting their 50-Year Golden Jubilee Celebration and had invited dignitaries from the Lutheran Church in Australia, Germany, Canada, and the United States. Because Lorraine had helped to start the work in Hong Kong, we were given VIP tags and bussed all over Hong Kong for three days of activities. As we drove, Lorraine told us her story.

❖ ❖ ❖

At the time Lorraine was first airlifted out of China, the mission board wanted to send all fleeing missionaries to India, but her team pleaded with the board. "The mission field is coming to us! Refugees are fleeing China and flooding into Hong Kong. We already speak their language, so we'd like to stay here and work with them." The mission board finally granted permission to open a school for the refugees.

Hong Kong is very mountainous with little usable land, so the sudden influx of refugees created a real crisis. Families camped in cardboard boxes along the streets and under stairways until the Hong Kong government built temporary tenement housing up the steep hillsides. The Lutheran Mission opened their first school on a tenement rooftop.

Rennie's Mill Camp (now *Tiu Keng Leng*) sprang up twenty miles outside the city with another huge gathering of refugees. The government granted space for the mission to build a chapel in the camp and one missionary moved there permanently to start a school.

❖ ❖ ❖

As we drove around the city visiting these sites, I was amazed at how the work of the mission had grown. Twenty-six elementary schools and six high schools now served the grandchildren of those refugees. Rennie's Mill Camp became a city! We went there to help dedicate a beautiful new Lutheran school in the heart of a cluster of six high-rise apartment buildings.

What impressed me most was the Martha Boss Community Center, named after one of the early missionaries. It stands eight stories high and was teeming with activity on the day we visited. Their "Cradle to Grave" ministry offers crafts for the kids, activities for the youth, programs for young families, and housing for the elderly.

Ben and Jacob arrived just in time to join us for the Jubilee Celebration on Sunday, where twelve thousand people filled the Hong Kong Coliseum. Lorraine was escorted onto the stage while we found seats in the bleachers and joined our hearts with the crowd for a fabulous celebration of praise to God for fifty years of grace and growth.

Lorraine was scheduled to speak that night at the Jubilee Banquet, and I had to chuckle when she told me her time allotment. The ministry had flown her 7000 miles as the only living missionary who helped start the work and then gave her three minutes to speak.

"How on earth can I cram ten years of history into three minutes?"

A fellow dignitary offered to share his time with her and encouraged her to talk as long as she needed. We figured they expected Lorraine to be a tottering old woman with a quivering voice. Instead, she spoke forcefully of the vision God had given them fifty years earlier. Her dynamic talk lasted twenty minutes and the people loved her.

At the same time, I was beginning to love the Chinese people. They were warm, friendly, and hospitable, and God was changing my attitude already by giving me a heart for the lovely Chinese Christians.

Unlike Lorraine, I am not the missionary type. If I have a ministry that I feel passionate about, it's my family. Little did I know that God was about to give me a gift that would expand my family and truly change my attitude forever. I simply needed to keep my heart open while I tagged along with our team through China and the gift would be revealed at the proper time.

Special Agent: Ben
Date: October 31, 1999
Location: Hong Kong
Event: The Jubilee Banquet

JAMES CHU: THE HAMBURGER MAN

I had jet lag and didn't know how much longer I could stay awake.

This is Ben again. My son Jacob and I had traveled nearly twenty-four hours on Saturday, and although the Jubilee Celebration Sunday afternoon was great, I wasn't pumped up for the evening banquet.

A waiter welcomed us into the hotel's huge banquet room filled with tables for twelve, and I looked around at 1400 faces as he led us to Aunt Lorraine's table. I was ready to eat but unlike our banquets in the United States, the speeches came before the food was served, while we were still hungry enough to listen. Aunt Lorraine spoke with such enthusiasm that I forgot about my stomach.

During dinner Aunt Lorraine introduced me to James Chu, the Chinese man sitting next to me. He wanted to know what had brought me to Hong Kong, and when I told him I was escorting my aunt into China he asked, "Is Miss White your aunt?" I nodded and he said, "I have a story to tell you. When I was a little boy, we lived in China. There were four in my family: my mother, father, brother, and myself. I was seven years old when the communists took over in 1949. They marched into our town with guns and killed my father. Mother snatched up the two of us boys and we fled to Hong Kong as refugees, but we had no place to stay. We lived under the stairway of an old building and spent each day trying to survive. One day, Miss White walked by and saw us under the steps and asked, 'Would you boys like to go to school?' We said, 'Sure, we'd love to go to school.' We went every day after that. When the weather got nasty, Miss White would say, 'It's going to rain tonight. Would you like to sleep in the school?' We'd say, 'Sure!' Then we would bring our mother, and we would all stay nice and dry. Ben, your aunt is a special lady. She helped us to get a new start in life!"

As James and I visited, I learned that he and his brother both graduated from the Lutheran school and went on to become successful businessmen. James Chu is the senior vice president over twenty-eight McDonald's restaurants in Southeast Asia. I quickly dubbed him **The Hamburger Man.** His brother became the senior vice president of a large banking conglomerate. His story was another fascinating example of abundant fruit fifty years after some small act of obedience to God's prompting. If Aunt Lorraine hadn't stopped to chat with those two boys under the stairway, their lives may have gone in totally different directions.

We began sharing as one businessman to another and as the conversation flowed, I was reminded of a principle. "James, when God spoke to Abraham and promised to bless him, it wasn't for Abraham's benefit only. It was a triangle of blessing. God said 'I will bless you so that you can be a blessing to others, and those people in turn will give Me the glory. Then, when I look down from heaven, I will see that the earth has yielded its produce.'" I shared with him how God had blessed our businesses and how we were trying to share that blessing with others. I explained how our business had adopted different nations in the world to become a blessing to them, so those people could come to know the Lord and give Him the praise and glory.

James was fascinated with this concept, so I invited him to a World Briefing where speakers share what God is doing around the world and offer opportunities to team up with their staff. "That's where we developed an eternal business plan for our companies. Their ministry enables busy men to make an impact on people's lives around the world for all eternity the same way Aunt Lorraine has touched your own life."

I asked him, "What more purpose can we find in life than to do something today that will have a positive impact on another person's life a thousand years from now?" James embraced the concept, and I suddenly realized that I no longer felt the slightest fatigue or jet lag. I was totally pumped up with the joy of imparting this vision to another successful businessman who could impact the lives of thousands that we ourselves would never be able to reach.

```
Special Agent: Lorraine
Date: November 2, 1999
Location: Chongqing, China
Event: Up the Yangtze River
```

CRAMMING SEVEN DAYS INTO SEVEN HOURS

What a strange-looking boat! Some thought it looked like a dinosaur, while others said it resembled a flying saucer. We stepped down into its enclosed belly and dropped our luggage next to a row of seats. The windows, barely a foot above the water, needed intense scrubbing and offered only a murky, impressionistic view of the outdoors.

I'm Ben's Aunt Lorraine, and as our hydrofoil boat sped away from the dock, I could see just enough of the countryside to remind me of another trip down this river fifty years earlier to renew my visa.

In 1948, when I was forced to wait six weeks for passage, the boat was packed like sardines with worried people. I could barely move and spent most days on my bunk listening to a sad couple quietly discuss their uncertain future in the strange-sounding tones of the Chinese language. On that trip, we met for meals in a central dining room, and I was shocked the first day when strangers took the liberty to use their own chopsticks to fill my bowl from the central dishes. I learned quickly that if I wanted to make my own selections I had better start scooping fast. Today, coolies (Chinese servants) came on board the boat at each village, offering hot food from their big bowls. But we preferred to eat our own power bars we'd brought from the U.S.

Today's trip was so different from my first journey. For one thing, we were traveling the opposite direction on the river. Last evening, we had flown into Chongqing, and this morning we were heading east down the river to Wanzhou City. Unlike the somber tone of my first journey in the midst of the communist situation, today we gained immediate passage, and our group felt happy and relaxed.

Peter, our guide and interpreter, had met us in Hong Kong yesterday, so the Rag-Tag Team was now complete. What fun! The atmosphere inside the boat sparkled with life. Ben and Peter told jokes. Cora, Jake, and I laughed. And everyone listened to my reminiscing. I was glad I had accepted Ben's offer to bring me back to China, and everyone felt the excitement and significance of my return.

My first trip up the river took seven days. Today's trip would take only seven hours in our speeding hydrofoil boat. We'd had breakfast in Chongqing, ate our sack lunches on the boat, and would arrive in Wanzhou City before dinner. As we grew closer to the city, I felt both anxious and excited. I wondered how things had changed since my first visit and how it was possible that thousands were coming to the Lord under communism. From what Ben told me, it sounded like God was doing mighty things and I was eager to see it for myself.

```
Special Agent: Lorraine
Date: November 2, 1999
Location: Rev. Zhang's Church
Event: Arrival in Wanzhou City
```

THE GREAT REUNION

"I remember these steps! This is where the coolies came and carried me up in a sedan chair." For a moment I was twenty-four years old again, seeing Miss Green waving from the dock. I remembered what a relief it had been to feel solid ground under my feet after seven days on a rocking boat. Then to eat good American food at the mission compound! That was incredible!

The sight greeting me today was totally different, except for the stairway—100 feet wide and 300 steps high, it created a grand entrance from the Yangtze River into Wanzhou City. Tall buildings lined the river on each side of the steps and continued upward row upon row until the huge city reached the top of the cliffs. A road intersected the steps one-third of the way up, and that's where we caught our cab.

We checked into a hotel to deposit our luggage and freshen up. I had asked Ben not to tell Rev. Zhang what time to expect us because I wanted to surprise him. It was mid-afternoon when we caught a cab to the church.

As soon as we arrived, word spread quickly, and the three assistant pastors rushed out to greet us. When I saw Rev. Zhang, he was so changed! He was a young newlywed in 1949, and now he was so old. But I was old too! We recognized each other immediately.

I will never forget that reunion. As we embraced, I felt I was hugging a friend who had returned from the grave. I had heard that Rev. Zhang lost his life during the Cultural Revolution, and until that moment, I secretly wondered if Ben was mistaken about his true identity. Although he had sent me pictures of himself, seeing was believing. What a joy to be together again! When I inquired about his wife and learned that she had been sick in bed for five years, we immediately went upstairs and laid hands on her and prayed. What an emotional time!

After serving us tea, the pastors took us on a tour. The Wan-Hsien I remembered was a country village with fields and gardens. Our little Lutheran Mission had four apartments with a lovely courtyard and a gardenia tree. There was nothing familiar about the Wanzhou City I was seeing today. I didn't recognize any houses or streets. The mission compound had vanished, and apartment buildings now stood on the site where it had been. Although the school was no longer Christian, I was astonished to learn that some in the relocated school knew about me. Other than the steps greeting us at the river, the only landmark I recognized was the big mountain peak looming over the city and welcoming me back.

```
Special Agent: Lorraine
Date: November 3, 1999
Location: New Church Sites
Event: A Significant Conversation
```

THAT DAM PROJECT & THE WANZHOU CHURCH SPLIT

China was building a dam. That may not seem like earth-shaking news, but for the people of Wanzhou City, it would change their lives forever.

Rev. Zhang and his assistants told us all about it on our second day of touring. In order to control flooding and provide irrigation, China had started to dam up the Yangtze River, building the largest dam in the world. He told us that when the dam was completed, hundreds of miles of the Yangtze River will stop flowing and create huge lakes. Three-Rivers Gorge—one of the Seven Wonders of the World—will be buried under water. The same fate awaited Wanzhou City, displacing over a million people.

Some changes come by choice, others by force. The church in Wanzhou City was about to experience a drastic change. This change falls into the second category—a forced change. Rev.

Zhang's church would be flooded. To complicate things, the congregation was scattered on each side of the river, and half of them crossed on bridges to attend church. When the river floods, the bridges will disappear, and the lake will be too wide to cross. In order to serve both halves of the congregation, the Wanzhou Church will have to split. That meant they needed to build not just one new church but two!

Rev. Zhang told us he had worked out an arrangement with the government to purchase new property. The officials promised to reimburse the congregation for the old church, but the amount will not cover the cost of two new buildings. As we drove to the new church sites with Rev. Zhang, I felt the Lord prompt my heart to help raise funds for this project. So much had already changed in the fifty years since my last visit to China, and I could see that God had shown Himself faithful to His Church through it all. I had no doubt that He would provide for them in the future.

I could scarcely believe that after fifty years of blind prayers, I had witnessed with my own eyes the fruit of our labors in Wan-Hsien, now called Wanzhou City. Once again, my heart was entwined with theirs and I decided to labor with them by raising support to build their new churches. What began as a simple visit to celebrate the past had grown into a passion to help them flourish in the future.

```
Special Agent: Jake
Date: November 3, 1999
Location: Wanzhou City
Event: Touring the High School
```

HOW IT FEELS TO BE A ROCK STAR

Seventeen hours on a plane to the middle of nowhere. Why am I doing this?

I'm Ben's son, Jake, and that's what was going through my mind the night before we left for China. When Dad first talked about taking Aunt Lorraine back to Wanzhou City, I was quick to say, "I'll go too!" I thought it would be a cool adventure into the wilderness of a foreign country. But when it came right down to packing the night before, I didn't really want to go anymore.

When we arrived in Hong Kong, I thought: *This isn't so bad. We stayed in a ritzy hotel, and it was nuts. Really nice!* China, however, was a different story. It was crazy but interesting. I didn't say much while we traveled. I pretty much just observed and tried to soak in the culture as we went up the river and when Rev. Zhang took Aunt Lorraine around to see her old stomping grounds. One of the reasons we came on this trip was to help the school celebrate their fifty-year anniversary, with Aunt Lorraine providing details about the first ten years as a Lutheran Mission School in Wanzhou.

The first thing I saw when we pulled into the driveway of the school was a big open area with a huge flower bed. Pretty soon the principal came out and several men took us to the big building on the left side of the compound. On the top (4th) floor, they showed us a museum-type room with historical pictures. That's when Aunt Lorraine told them about the school before the Cultural Revolution.

Next, they took us into an empty classroom where the old people could talk. I got bored and decided to sneak out to walk around, and I noticed a bunch of girls looking down at me from a balcony. I have light hair which they don't see too often in China. I waved up at them and they started screaming just like I was a rock star. I thought, *Whoa, this is cool!* I waved again and they screamed again. That was pretty fun! The old people came out just in time to hear them scream, and my dad thought it was really funny.

We walked down to the athletic field just when the girl's gym class ended. The girls huddled into a group and pointed at me. I just grinned. Finally, one girl got up enough courage to walk over to us. She was so nervous that her chin quivered when she spoke.

"Do you like Michael Jackson?"

I said, "No."

"Do you like Mariah Carey?"

Again, I said, "No."

I wasn't quite as nervous as she was, but I didn't know what to say. It was pretty funny.

I thought about that experience on the way back to the hotel and remembered something Dad had talked about, but which had remained a mystery to me until that moment: *The power of influence.* Those girls didn't know me from Adam, and they certainly weren't screaming because of anything special I had done. I just happened to be an American high school kid with light hair which placed me in a position of influence. I could have used it either for good or for bad. The choice was up to me. At the time, I didn't have a clue what to say. But as I thought about it, I began to catch a vision for how I might be able to use my influence in a positive way in the future. God says, "Always be ready to give an answer for the hope that is within you" (1 Peter 3:15). Next time, I'll be ready!

Special Agent: Ben
Date: November 3, 1999
Location: Wanzhou City
Event: Another Banquet

101 WAYS TO WOK YOUR DOG

This is Ben again, and we were sitting in the finest traditional restaurant in Wanzhou City. Why else would Rev. Zhang and his assistants take us there for our farewell dinner?

We were escorted to a special room set aside for groups and were seated once again at a large round table spread with exotic foods. Later, we affectionately referred to this meal as our "24-course high-protein banquet." If you had been with us and were looking at these dishes, which ones would you choose to eat?

- Cooked snake
- Fried eel
- Chicken feet
- Rooster combs
- Cow stomach
- Pig's tails
- Pig's ears

- Ground nuts
- Squid
- Shrimp
- Crab
- Snails
- Fish blubber
- Fish air sacks
- Turtle soup with head and feet still on the turtle
- Duck tongue—little one-inch tongues with long skinny muscles that look like wishbones, served with hot sauce.
- Peking Duck—the server brings a beautifully browned duck to the table for you to admire. Then he disappears with it and returns with just the skin that has been cut into little squares. You take the squares, put them into little round tortillas and spread them with black paste. It looks like baby poop but is actually quite tasty. Then you roll it all up and that's Peking Duck. We kept wondering: *Where's the meat?*
- Black Chicken Soup—a whole chicken with head and feet. The chicken is black, the bones are black, and broth is black. It's cooked long and slow so that when you reach in with your chopsticks to get some of the chicken, it pulls right off the bones.
- Cooked lettuce
- Cooked vegetables
- Fresh vegetables—we were warned not to eat raw

vegetables because our systems are not accustomed to Chinese amoebas, so these were not an option.

One of Jake's goals for his China adventure was to eat dog. When we inquired at this restaurant, the server said, "Oh, you can't get dog here. If you want really good dog, you have to go up to Manchuria." We decided to remember that the next time we visited Esther!

Date: November 4, 1999
Location: Yangtze River
Event: Return Trip

DEVIL CITY

"Check it out, Dad." Jake pointed out the window of the boat. "It looks like somebody toilet-papered the mountain."

I looked where Jake was pointing and saw what seemed to be white canvas zigzagging back and forth up the mountainside toward a tall formation. As the boat drew closer, we could clearly see a huge head that stood at least five stories high and wore a flat-topped hat with striped ear flaps. The eyes were closed, and the mouth frowned. Below it all, a drab city lay nestled along the riverbank.

"Peter, could you find out what that is?" I asked. He questioned a fellow passenger and then told us the story of that strange place.

"They call it Devil City. The head at the top is a Buddhist temple. What we see going up the mountain are canvas tunnels that lead the people from one station to the next, representing eighteen different levels of hell. One level shows a person tied onto a rack with a cross-cut blade slowly sawing him in half, but of course, he never dies. Another level shows someone hung upside down from a waterwheel that slowly dips him into the water to drown, then pulls him out just long enough to catch his breath before dropping him under again. This goes on forever. The snake pit is for those who fear vipers. The person runs forever through poisonous snakes without ever finding a way out. The purpose of Devil City is to give people a picture of hell, thus encouraging them to live good lives."

"You mean they scare the hell right out of 'em?" Jake asked.

Peter nodded. "That's pretty much how it is. You'd never know if your life was good enough until you died, and then it would be too late."

"We are so blessed to know that we don't have to worry like that," Lorraine said. "I'm so grateful Jesus died on the cross to pay the penalty for our sins!"

Mom chimed in. "It must be hard living in that kind of fear."

A short distance down the river, as our boat turned toward the shore to pick up more passengers, I happened to look out just as a dead man's body floated past us in the middle of the river. When I had recovered from my shock, I wondered how the man came to be in the river. Had he been murdered? Or had he perhaps visited Devil's City and felt so tormented by his failures that he committed suicide? What kind of struggles might he have faced as he tried to live a good enough life to get to heaven? He was up against terrible odds because, in his own power, there was no way to overcome the temptations of the devil.

Over the years I've heard people ask: "Who do you think you are, trying to change the happy pagans? They're fine just the way they are." The sight of that dead man floating in the water had a profound impact on me. What makes people think the pagans are so happy? That man may have been consumed with fear.

I realized at that moment that *people need Jesus.* They need the *peace* of mind that comes with knowing Jesus died to save them. They need the *power* of the Holy Spirit to overcome the temptations of the devil. They need the *assurance* of knowing they've been adopted into God's family and that He is preparing a special place for them in heaven when they cross over to the other side of *that* river.

Devil City made me keenly aware of our deep spiritual need. People know they sin and deserve punishment. Many live in fear. If only they could meet the Savior who took their punishment upon Himself so they could be set free!

```
Special Agent: Cora
Date: November 5, 1999
Location: Hong Kong Airport
Event: Goodbye to Peter
```

GRANDMA GETS HER GIFT

This is Cora again. I had prayed that God would change my attitude, and He had answered my prayer. My week in Asia gave me a deep love and appreciation for the Chinese people. Sometimes when God answers our prayers, He says, "Yes, and here's more!" I didn't know it, but today was going to be one of those times.

Our trip was ending. Going through Customs was not my favorite thing to do. It's a long and tiring process. In this case, it also marked the end of our time with Peter since he was flying home to Singapore.

Before coming to China, I had heard so much about Peter through Ben that I felt like I knew him before we ever met. On the day we arrived in China, I had watched Ben give Peter a hello hug and I thought: *If Ben can hug him, so can I!* To my surprise, he stiffened and pulled away. Later I learned that Chinese men and women never embrace in public. After a week of traveling together, Peter now seemed like one of the family. As we stood in line, he turned to me and said, "When we met five days ago, you told me to call your sister 'Aunt Lorraine,' but you never told me what to call you. I'll just call you 'Mom.'"

"That's okay. I have a Chinese daughter who also calls me Mom." I told him about Alice, the only other Chinese person I had ever known. A new arrival from Hong Kong, Alice had met my daughter Ruth at college and Ruth brought her home for Christmas break. It didn't take long to see that Alice felt lost and alone, so we embraced her as a part of our family and because her mother had died when Alice was just a child, she soon started calling me "Mom."

I said to Peter, "Now that you also call me 'Mom,' I have both a Chinese daughter and a Chinese son."

Peter smiled. "Does Alice have any children?"

When I said no, he announced: "Well, now you not only have a Chinese son, but a Chinese daughter-in-law and four Chinese grandchildren!"

What a precious gift! The Lord instantly added six members to my family, and they were all Chinese. Not only did He fill my heart with love, but He said, "Yes, and here's more!"

ASSIGNMENT DEBRIEFED (BEN)

FINANCES! Must you be wealthy in order to give? Could it be possible to simply position yourself as a conduit of God's blessings to others?

As young businessmen, we began our adventure in giving

by tithing the traditional ten percent of our income to our local church. Then I read a book by R.G. LeTourneau, founder of a large heavy equipment company, who turned those numbers around. He kept 10 percent of his income and invested 90 percent into God's work! The book taught me that giving is not limited to a certain percentage. Since that time, God has blessed our businesses, enabling us to increase our giving several times over. We still have a long way to go to reach LeTourneau's goal, but our hearts are headed in that direction.

Here are some interesting principles that we learned about giving:

- It's not a matter of having enough money, but of strategically placing the money that you have.
- The Triangle of Blessing says that when God blesses us, He desires us to use those blessings to bless others who will in turn give Him the praise.

Our China trip also taught me some things beyond Finances that I would like to share as well.

Aunt Lorraine's story showed me that *a small act of obedience today can yield great fruit in the future.* God led us to Wanzhou City to show us the fruit of Aunt Lorraine's obedience in becoming a missionary and also praying for fifty years. Having seen the impact of her kindness to the Hamburger Man in Hong Kong and to the little girl in Wanzhou City who later discipled others, I felt that God had not only placed His stamp of approval on our commitment to China, He had also helped us envision what our investment could result in fifty years down the road. It was as though He told us, "Keep going. You're on the right track." This story will encourage me until the day I die.

Another principle comes to mind as I ponder our China adventure: *"Never doubt in the darkness what God has shown you in the light!"* In the midst of a struggle, it's easy to doubt whether or not you're on the right track. When I was in the midst of culture shock and said I would never return, I was doubting that God had really led us to China. Then I remembered a story I once heard about a missionary in the days of Marco Polo. He was crossing the desert in a camel caravan when a windstorm came up and he had to hunker down behind the camels for two days. It was dark under that blanket! The missionary had strange thoughts and wondered if he should forsake His call to mission work. After that experience he always said, "Don't doubt in the darkness what God has shown you in the light!"

In the years following our China faith-pledge, we saw God channel His blessings through our business in ways we could never have imagined. The following winter, my brother Jim got the idea of transforming returned concrete into jumbo blocks for retaining walls. God then gave us the insight to make the blocks look like natural rock, which created a new niche market in the concrete industry. We started a new business called Redi-Rock International and as a result of God's inspiration and blessing, we were not only able to fulfill our pledge but to develop new relationships with hundreds of manufacturers and employees, expanding our influence around the world. My three children now run that business with Jake as president. He's become a whole new kind of rock star!

God enabled us to give above and beyond all that we had pledged. God used that experience to expand our faith as we positioned ourselves to see His mighty hand at work in China. We developed a deeper purpose for our business when we earmarked the profits for our partner ministries.

Over the years we have also experienced seasons of financial setbacks when we were not able to give to the levels we had hoped. God used those times to keep us humble and remind us that this is His business. As He provides, we will give.

Could God be calling you to experience this kind of adventure? Can you imagine yourself making a faith pledge to a specific project and watching Him provide?

GRANDMA GETS HER GIFT | 189

A Divine Appointment

A Family Treasure Found

Cramming Seven Days into Seven Hours

Two White Haired Grandmas
Lorraine & Cora

The Great Reunion

LaVia de Lorraina

GRANDMA GETS HER GIFT | 191

4TH ASSIGNMENT—
"E" is for Expertise

Special Agent Ben's Assignment to Colombia

Your assignment, should you choose to accept it, is to go to Medellin, Colombia and determine whether or not your business team will partner with the ministry team in Medellin.

You will be part of an investigative group who will travel with Pablo and evaluate his strategy in terms of your own goals.

You will be escorted by Layo Leiva, Assistant Director of Campus Crusade for Christ for Latin America, and Mike Fleetwood, Liason for History's Handful.

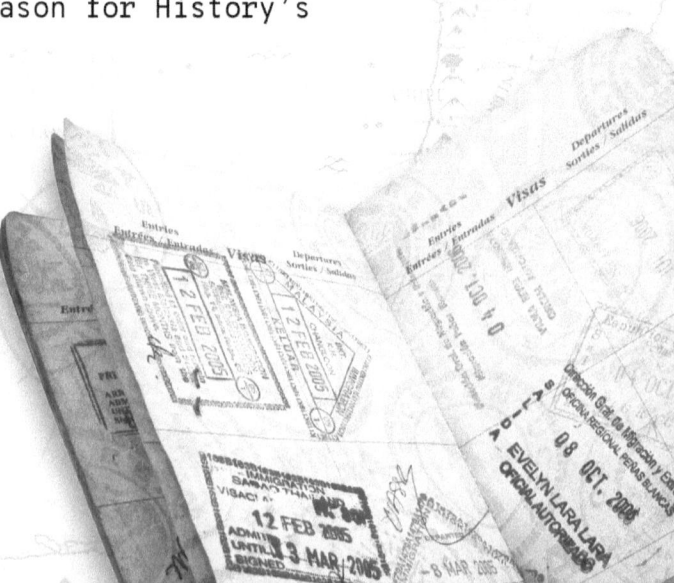

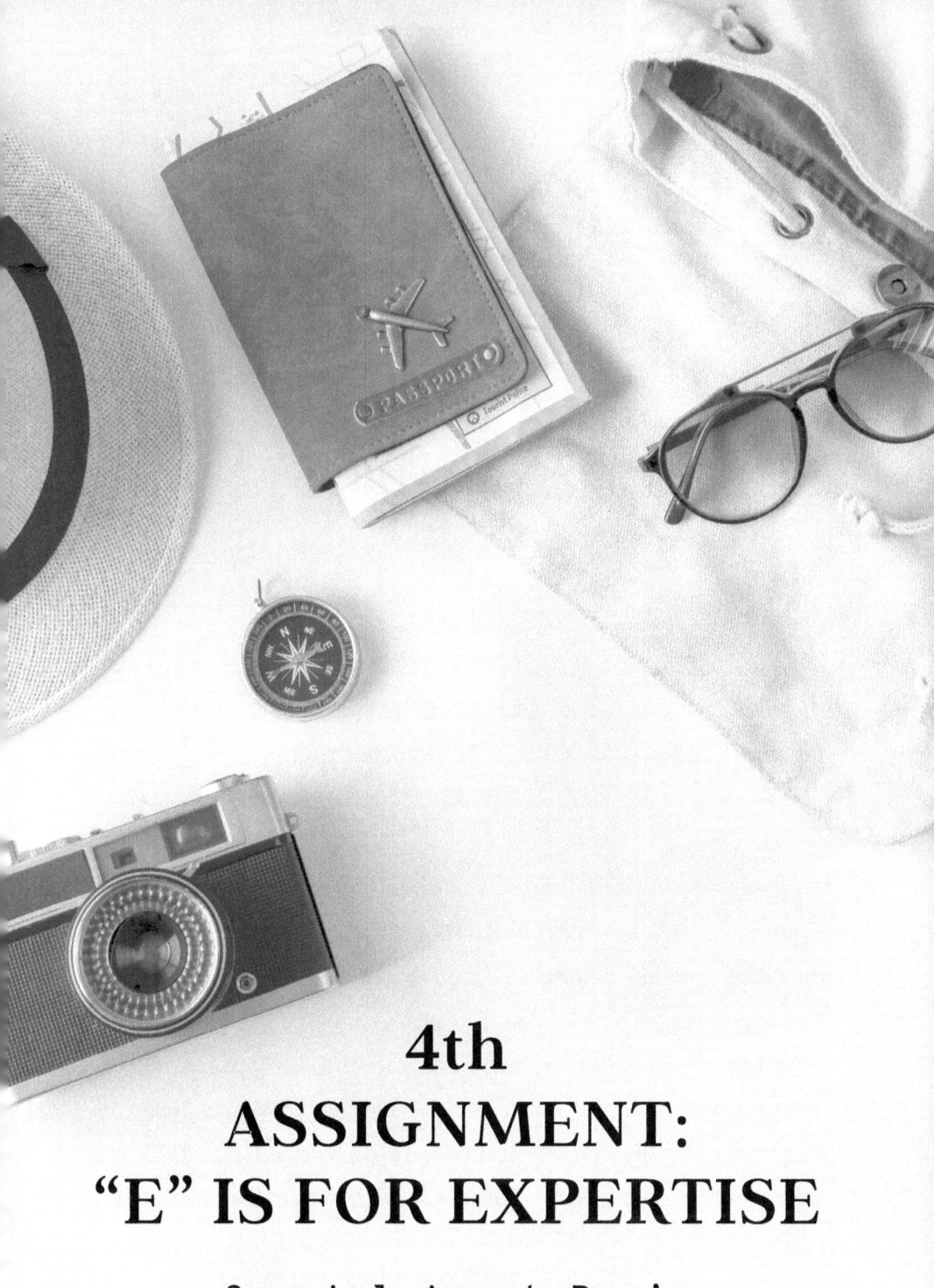

4th ASSIGNMENT: "E" IS FOR EXPERTISE

Special Agent Ben's Assignment to Colombia

```
Date: August 1997
Location: Our Corporate Offices
Event: A Conference Call
```

FORREST GUMP OR INDIANA JONES?

It's fun to imagine ourselves like Indiana Jones, out on the cutting edge. The truth is, being an "Indiana Jones" takes a tremendous amount of courage. More often than not, we've been like Forrest Gump—we just happened to be in the right place at the right time.

Today we gathered around our conference room table where Tom had called an impromptu meeting. I recognized the voice over the speaker phone as Layo Leiva, assistant director of Campus Crusade for Christ in South America. We had worked with Layo in El Salvador, and I enjoyed him immensely.

Last week we had spoken with Layo at the World Briefing and, more out of curiosity than anything, we had asked, "If we were to adopt a country in South America, where would you like to see us get involved?"

His answer came in a flash: "Medellin, Colombia!"

We recognized the city right away. Medellin was home to the late drug lord, Pablo Escobar.

Although we loved Latin America, we had recently committed to adopt the Sichuan Province of China. We told Layo about our faith pledge and said, we're already in over our heads, but if nobody else takes Medellin, give us a call and we will strongly consider it."

A week had passed and now Layo was calling. "Gentlemen, you're not going to believe what happened. Every single South American need we presented was adopted except for one city in Colombia. Would you still consider taking Medellin?"

We looked at each other and shrugged. Then Tom leaned forward and said: "I'll tell you what, Layo. If you can arrange for us to travel into Colombia and visit your staff, we'll check it out. If the Lord plants Colombia in our hearts while we're there, then we will adopt Medellin."

Could it be that we were becoming like Forrest Gump once again?

```
Date: Six months later
Location: Ben's house
Event: A Telephone Conversation
```

SURE, I'D LIKE TO VISIT JUAN VALDEZ

I had carried the TV commercial picture of Juan Valdez on the coffee bean wagon in my imagination for six months now and thought: *Colombia! What a great place to go!*

My first clue that Colombia might be something altogether different came when I called our travel agent to book the flight. "What's with you guys?" she had asked. "While everyone else travels to exotic places like Tahiti, you go to the most dangerous countries in the world!"

I chuckled and said, "Ann, we are the ones going to the most exotic places on the planet. We go where the action is… where the real people live!" But inside I was thinking: *Did she say dangerous?*

I mentioned her comment to the others, and we decided to call General Abel who had connections with the Pentagon and could check into the Colombia situation. His secretary put us through to him and I explained our situation. His voice betrayed his deep concern as he said, "When I was in active duty, I was forced to fly into harm's way. Now that I'm retired, I do not travel into countries like Colombia where the State Department has issued a warning. If anything were to happen to you, the United States government could not get you out. Our hands would be tied. But if you decide to go, Ben, I will pray for you."

I thought back to our Mongolian adventure and wondered: *What are we getting ourselves into this time?*

My mental picture of Colombia was quickly changing from Juan Valdez to a place of hidden hostility.

Did we dare to go?

Date: November 1997
Location: Petoskey, MI
Event: Breakfast at Flap Jack

A STRANGE & FUNNY MEETING

We were scheduled to leave in a week, yet here we were at the Flap Jack Restaurant for a breakfast meeting—trying to decide whether or not to go.

Since I had called the meeting, Tom looked at me and said, "Ben, what have you got? What's bothering you?" (To be honest, I was looking for someone to cancel this crazy trip!)

Being the youngest in a family business with six strong-willed partners can tend to keep you humble. In spite of the risk that they might consider me a pansy, I felt a responsibility to express my concerns.

"Did you guys watch the news last night?" They shook their heads. "A geologist from a Canadian company was kidnapped by terrorists in **Colombia**! They'd held him hostage for several weeks while the owner of the company tried to negotiate his release. Last night, the report showed the owner walking up to the terrorists on a mountain trail in Colombia for a swap. The employee walked away to freedom while the owner was taken into custody by a terrorist group called the FARC."

I reminded them of General Abel's warning and added, "Two nights ago I woke up in the middle of the night in a cold sweat saying: *What am I getting myself into?* Maybe it was a warning from God. I asked Nancy to do some research on the internet." I reached into my briefcase and pulled out the article. "Here's what she found:

> **WARNING:** There is a greater risk of being kidnapped in Colombia than in any other country in the world…. In some cases, the victims have been murdered. Most kidnappings of U.S. citizens in Colombia have been committed by guerrilla groups, including the Revolutionary Armed Forces of Colombia (FARC) and the National Liberation Army (ELN), which were both designated as Foreign Terrorist Organizations by the Secretary of State… Since it is U.S. policy not to pay ransom or make other concessions to terrorists, the U.S. Government's ability to assist kidnapped U.S. citizens is limited."

I looked up from reading and saw fear in Mark's eyes that matched my own. Then I told them that another report listed Colombia's terrorist groups as the "Most Likely to Succeed" in the whole world.

"Here's how it works. You arrive at Immigration, and they take your passport into the back room, promising to return it to you when you leave the country. Then they call their terrorist friends and inform them of your arrival, at which time you become a target for the kidnappers who now have your picture and know your itinerary."

"How do they kidnap people?" Mark asked.

"Well, I guess a lot of Americans go into night clubs and the terrorists slip stuff into their drinks to knock them out. Another tactic they use is they dress up like policemen and stop you for your credentials. If your passport was confiscated at the airport, they say, 'You must come in for questioning.' If you won't come, one of them holds up a newspaper like he's reading and then inhales special smoke from a pipe that he blows in your face to lower your resistance."

I searched their faces and said, "American businessmen are the prime target for the world's 'Most Likely to Succeed' terrorist group. Do you still think we should go?"

Mark asked, "What does Nancy think?"

He knew that my wife and I had made an agreement when I first began traveling that I would never go without her wholehearted support. Every missions trip is a team effort—she stays with the kids and prays while I go out into the world.

I cringed at Mark's question and had to tell him the truth. I had expected Nancy to put her foot down and veto the trip. Instead, just this morning Nancy had said, "Ben, I've prayed, and I am not going to tell you whether or not to go on this trip. You need to obey whatever you believe God is leading you to do."

Nancy wasn't giving me any way out and now I was hoping Mark and Tom would see the danger and decide to cancel the trip. I looked at Mark with hopeful eyes and finally he spoke the words I had been waiting to hear: "I don't think it would be fair to my family to put myself into that much danger. Count me out!"

We both looked at Tom, but he had that determined look he gets when no amount of convincing will sway him from his convictions. "You two can stay, but I intend to go even if I have to crawl down there on my hands and knees. We made a commitment, and I believe we are called to go."

I balked at his words. "What about the danger? What about the terrorists?"

Tom leaned forward and spread his hands on the table. "Guys, let me tell you what I learned in Mongolia. It's a lesson I've been working on for several years, and this is my opportunity to apply it."

He leaned back and settled into his chair to tell us the story…

"Ben, do you remember when we were in Mongolia and that teacher named Doug said, 'Obedience is more important than safety?' "

Of course, I remembered.

Tom looked me in the eye and said, "Ben, I've been thinking about that concept for a long time, mulling it over in my mind. At first, I felt guilty and small in my own approach to life because I was looking at safety as my primary concern while Doug was focusing on obedience. This is my opportunity to follow his example. If God is opening the door for us to go to Colombia, then I'm going!"

Mark and I were still ambivalent. Tom said, "I know this is a new concept for you. How about if we go over to the office and call Layo to discuss your concerns? Then you guys can pray about it over the weekend, and we'll meet again Monday morning to make our final decisions."

We adjourned to the conference room at the office. Maybe Layo would have the sense to tell us to stay home.

But no! Layo said: "Men, one thing I have learned in my travels is to depend on our people on the ground. If they tell me that it's okay to come, I trust them. I've called down to Colombia, and they assured me that they have arranged for our security and will take us only to places that are safe. Would you mind if I pray with you over the phone?" We gave our consent and Layo prayed that God would enable us to shift our focus from personal safety to the people whose lives would be changed forever by our visit.

I felt my focus begin to shift, but still I wanted to pray about it over the weekend. So far, no doors had closed, and I couldn't see any biblical principle we were violating by going. The only thing holding me back was my own fear.

That Sunday morning, as I was teaching Philippians 4 in Sunday School, verses 6-7 seemed to jump out at me:

> *Be anxious for nothing, but in everything by prayer and supplication with thanksgiving let your requests be made known to God. And the peace of God, which surpasses all comprehension, shall guard your hearts and your minds in Christ Jesus.*

As I started teaching the lesson, I thought: ***Surely this doesn't apply to a life-and-death situation like Colombia!*** But by the end of the lesson, I realized the terrible truth. If I couldn't apply God's Word to the Colombia situation, then it would never mean a thing to me for the rest of my life. I needed to trust God enough to be willing to go.

Monday morning, I woke up with one strong conviction in my mind. Tom should not go alone. When we reconvened for our breakfast meeting at the Flap Jack, Tom was more convinced than ever that he was called to go.

I said, "The only thing I know for certain is that Tom should not go alone. If Mark goes, I'll stay."

Mark said, "I've decided to stay."

I responded, "Then I feel I should go."

So, Mark said, "If you and Tom are both going, then I'll go too."

I said, "Mark, if you want to go, that's great! Then I'll stay."

Mark said, "No, if you stay, I'm staying. If you go, I'll go."

For me, it was a no-win situation. Neither Nancy nor Mark were giving me a way out.

Tom shook his head. "You guys evaluate things very differently than I do!"

It was true. My criteria said that two people had to go. Mark's criteria said that if I went, he would go and if I stayed, he would stay. Tom simply said, "Obedience is more important than safety, so I'm going!"

Tom then reminded us of the lives of the apostles, who went wherever God sent them despite the dangers. Most were martyred for sharing the gospel. Saint Paul certainly did not choose his itineraries according to safety: He was shipwrecked three times, stoned in several cities, thrown into prison, and eventually killed. Even though he knew he would face death in Rome, he went because he knew God wanted him to go.

The time had come for me to focus on God's purposes, "that no one should perish but that all should come to repentance" (2 Peter 3:9) and put the fear and dangers behind my back just as Layo had prayed.

Elisabeth Elliot once said: "A whole lot of what we call 'struggling' is simply *delayed obedience*."

The struggle was over. My focus had shifted from the concern of safety to the task God was *calling* us to do. By the end of that strange and funny meeting, I knew I was going to Colombia!

Date: December 1997
Location: Medellin, Colombia
Event: Arrival in Colombia

RUNNING THE GAUNTLET AT THE COLOMBIAN AIRPORT

The dictionary defines the phrase "running the gauntlet" as: *(1) A double line of men armed with clubs with which to beat a person forced to run between them; (2) An ordeal in which one comes under fire from several quarters.*

My mind ran wild with a picture of "running the gauntlet" at the Colombia airport: **Customs officials confiscating our passports…getting bumped and robbed by the crowd outside the airport…nasty bad guys with guns waiting to whisk us away in their 4-wheel-drive Land Rovers, etc.**

Our Colombia-bound jet jostled a bit in the turbulence, and I feared that upon landing, I was about to become Indiana Jones whether I liked it or not. My hands grew clammy, and I felt myself slipping into an anxiety attack. Suddenly, General Abel's parting words popped into my head.

"If things start getting tense, Ben, just remember 9-1-1!"

The conversation replayed itself in my mind.

General Abel had said, "When we find ourselves in trouble here in America, we call 9-1-1, right?"

"Yes."

"Well, if you're ever in trouble down in Colombia, just read Psalm 91:1. It's the psalm of protection that I prayed before every mission I flew into Vietnam."

I looked the passage up and read it to my family before I left home.

> *He who dwells in the secret place of the Most High shall abide in the shadow of the Almighty God.*
> *I will say of the Lord, He is my Refuge and my fortress:*
> *My God, in Him will I trust.*
> *Surely He will deliver me...*
> *A thousand may fall at your side,*
> *And ten thousand at your right hand;*
> *But it shall not come near you.*

That psalm was my final confirmation that we were doing the right thing by going, and now it calmed my nerves as we approached Medellin.

Knowing that foreign businessmen were the targets of terrorist groups, we grew beards hoping to blend in with the unsavory types. But we didn't know that Colombian men don't have beards! The minute we stepped into the airport, children pointed at us and shouted, "Gringo! Gringo!" At that moment I would have liked to sink into the floor. Unfortunately, I was way too tall, too white, and too American to vanish into the crowd!

My eyes quickly scanned the crowd looking for "thugs, kidnappers, and nasty bad men," as one article had described them. Instead, families greeted one another with hugs and kisses, and friendly faces smiled at us.

Still, my guard was up. That morning, I'd packed all my essentials into a small backpack and made sure I wore running shoes. I'd joked with a friend back home that, "If they come after us, I'll just drop my pack and run!" to which my friend had responded, "you'll never be able to outrun the banditos." I had said, "I don't need to. I just need to outrun Mark and Tom. Then they'll get caught and I won't!" A smile sneaked out as I prepared to sprint if necessary.

Our walk through the airport was anticlimactic. The customs officials looked casually at our passports, handed them back, and waved us on toward the exit where Pablo and his people stood waiting. They tossed our luggage into the trunk and hustled us into the van.

I had no idea that 'running the gauntlet' could be so easy.

Date: December, 1997
Location: Streets of Medellin
Event: Trip from Airport to Hotel

DRUG HIT MAN, A.K.A. OUR BODY GUARD

There was no time for introductions. Fortunately, most of our team already knew each other from previous encounters. I looked around the car and sized up our team.

Mike Fleetwood	Liaison between businessmen in History's Handful and the National Director of the country being visited. Mike made sure all our questions were answered.
Layo Leiva	Assistant Area Director for Latin America Campus Crusade for Christ
Pablo Cano	National Director of Colombia Campus Crusade for Christ
Claudia Cano	Pablo's wife and assistant

I looked at Mark and Tom and saw that they were eyeing our driver suspiciously. Once I thought about it, the way he was driving made me wonder if we had truly escaped the terrorists after all. He did have an unsavory look about him. I wondered: *Have we been kidnapped already?* Within seconds the speedometer registered sixty and we were still inside the city. Then I noticed that he never stopped at the stop signs. In fact, he glanced both directions and accelerated.

Pablo and Layo both looked so peaceful, and I thought: *Certainly their faces would register anxiety if something were amiss!* Just then Tom leaned over to Pablo, nodded toward the driver, and said something. When Pablo answered, Tom smiled.

"What did he say, Tom? What's happening?" I asked. That's when we learned about the newest member of our team.

Manuel, our driver and bodyguard, was a former hitman for the drug cartel!

We couldn't see much of the city at that speed and before long, Manuel slammed on the brakes in front of a fenced-in hotel, made a quick turn, and spoke hurriedly to the gatekeeper. The gates swung open, and we were suddenly inside the hotel grounds which were patrolled to ensure the safety of the clients.

"You can relax now, men," Layo said. "You're safe!"

Inside the hotel, we were formally introduced to our driver. That was an adventure in itself. Manuel was short, muscular, and very intense. I felt a bit strange and awed by his background with the drug mafia. We learned that Manuel had recently met Jesus through the ministry of Pablo's team in Medellin and he was now our brother in Christ.

Manuel became our special friend that week. He told us that he intentionally sped through the intersections because when you stop, that's when you become vulnerable to attack. He knew exactly how the terrorists operated, and his eyes were trained to be vigilant on our behalf.

Isn't it amazing how God works? He orchestrated this blessing in such a way that Manuel not only got saved but also knew how to keep us safe.

```
Date: Later that week
Location: The Old Hacienda
          Restaurant
Event: Lunch
```

A PLAN UNFOLDS

The week had sped by in a flurry of activity.

Today was our final day in Medellin, and Pablo wanted to debrief us about the ministry. He took us to lunch at The Old Hacienda Restaurant, and we had just finished eating when somebody knocked over some shot glasses and they rolled across the table, landing in Tom's lap.

"You'd better write this in your journal, Ben," Tom laughed. "Suddenly, out of nowhere, there was a shot… glass rolling across the table!"

We had not seen a single "thug" the whole week, and by now we were joking about the dangers we had feared. Manuel had kept us very safe while we visited house churches, met the staff, and built special relationships.

"What was your favorite memory, Ben?" Claudia asked.

"Hmm… My favorite memory would have to be the night of the JESUS film."

Pablo had taken us out to a village on the mountainside one

night, and we had set up a huge movie screen in the park. The poor who live in their barrios (slums) surrounding the city have little access to electricity, so for many of them, the opportunity to watch a movie was a big event. Within thirty minutes, a tightly packed crowd filled the area, and the children in the front row sat stone-still, mesmerized by the story. They watched Jesus heal the sick and raise the dead, and when the angry mob demanded that Jesus be crucified, tears streamed down their cheeks and they yelled, "No! Don't kill him!!" Afterwards, many people asked Jesus into their hearts and lives.

Claudia then turned to Tom. "What stands out to you?"

"Besides the incredible beauty of the country, the thing that had impressed me the most is the Colombian people, especially your staff. They say it's hard to find a good employee these days. We've experienced the truth of that in the States, although we've been blessed with some excellent employees in our businesses. But if our team is great, your team is incredible!" Tom turned toward Pablo. "Your people have loving hearts and warm smiles, but they are also very committed and focused on their goals."

"Speaking of goals," Mark said to Pablo, "I'm very impressed with your plan for reaching Medellin. A wise man once said, 'Plan your work and work your plan.' Your team is truly following that motto."

Tom agreed. "How about if you lay out your plan one more time for us so we can present your goals accurately to the guys back home."

Pablo nodded. "Let me think a moment about how I can give you the fullest picture…"

Pablo paused for a moment and then launched into his story.

"Our plan began with a problem. It's important that you understand that the original strategy of Campus Crusade for Christ International was to share Jesus with university students who would become the future leaders of the nation. Once those students were taught Biblical truths and trained in how to share those truths with others, we encouraged them to plug into their local church in order to reach the community. That's where they ran into a problem. South America is predominantly Catholic, and unfortunately, the priests told the students to stop working with our ministry. We saw a lot of frustrated, fired-up students sitting in the pews doing nothing.

"We evaluated the problem and decided that we needed a new strategy here in Colombia to harness the spiritual energy of these young people. We did some brainstorming and finally settled on a solution. We needed to start our own churches. This required a policy change within Campus Crusade for Christ International, and it took some convincing.

"You see, it's very important that we work alongside the church. We believe it's wrong to say, 'Don't go to your church anymore. Come to ours.' You can't just tell people to throw away everything they've learned and do things our way. That would be difficult and divisive. It would be like telling them to stop being Colombian!

"Instead, we began to hold our meetings on Saturday and

encouraged the students to attend Mass on Sunday. Our goal was not to draw them away from the Catholic Church but to make sure they got fed, taught the Bible, and had opportunities to share Jesus in their city."

"We now have 16 churches in Medellin. We're focusing on reaching the entire community for Christ in five years. Our short-term goal is to multiply and have 50 churches across the city in the next two years."

Tom leaned forward. "Pablo, what can we do to help your ministry? What do you need from us?"

Pablo smiled. "I was hoping you would ask. First, I think our citywide outreach would be more effective if we could advertise on the radio and television to let people know who we are and why we will be visiting them. Second, I'd love to host some citywide celebrations in the Coliseum during Christmas and Easter. Unfortunately, we have to pay for facilities and airtime. Colombia is going through a recession right now and our people are struggling financially. We would need outside help for these ideas to become a reality."

Claudia nodded in a way that caught my eye, and I said, "Claudia, what are you thinking?"

She said, "I'm thinking about our reputation as drug lords. Medellin's past has brought tears to the eyes of the Colombians, but our hope and prayer is that in the future, the city of Medellin will export God's love throughout our country and even to the rest of the world."

Our group grew silent as we absorbed those words.

Mark broke the silence. "So, if we decided to adopt Medellin, your dreams of reaching the entire city could become a reality?"

"Absolutely! Depending on how much became available, we could accomplish those two goals and possibly even set up more training centers where new Christians could come to pick up literature and receive discipleship training. They could then share Christ with their friends and neighbors. **And** we could recruit new staff teams to show the JESUS film throughout Colombia."

"Is there anything else you've been cooking up in that creative mind of yours?" Tom asked playfully.

Pablo grinned. "There is one more thing… Actually, it's not an idea yet. Just a thought—a concern."

We waited.

"Here's the situation. Most missionaries focus their efforts on reaching the poor people of the nation who are in desperate need of hope and who are often more receptive to hearing the Gospel message. That's what you saw in the village where we showed the JESUS film. But to reach the city and the nation, I'm not sure that's the best way to accomplish our goals. It's one thing to challenge the poor in a nation; but to challenge the leadership—that's where decisions are made that influence the poor. I'm thinking it would be a good idea to connect with the business community, but I'm not sure how to go about doing that…"

That captured my attention. I love brainstorming! We tossed around several ideas. Should we invite a high-profile astronaut to speak to them? Or an athlete? Or a politician?

Pablo shook his head. "Right now, when our biggest industry

in Colombia is kidnapping foreigners for ransom, it would be unwise to bring down any high-profile people. I think what would be most effective is if you men, as American businessmen, would come back and challenge our businessmen. The Colombians would be very interested to know what makes Americans successful."

Tom picked up on the idea immediately. "We could address the following questions: *What motivates us in our work? Why do we get involved in Great Commission efforts?*"

Pablo nodded excitedly. "There's another benefit. It would bring tremendous credibility to our movement if you would align yourselves with our ministry."

The hour passed quickly as we hatched out a plan to create a business seminar. Through that discussion, Tom, Mark, and I could see that it was not only important but crucial that we team up with Pablo at this time.

"Besides," Pablo added, "you're the only ones who have the heart and courage to come. We have invited many other businessmen, but they all refused because of the danger."

I shook my head. "We must be the dumbest ones of all!"

We laughed, but I felt profoundly grateful to Tom for his deep conviction that *obedience is more important than safety*. We would have missed out on an incredible blessing if we had chosen to stay at home.

```
Date: The next day
Location: Medellin
Event: Returning to the U.S.A
```

LEAVING OUR HEARTS IN COLOMBIA

On the way back to the airport, our new friends took us on a scenic drive through a neighborhood that was guarded, and we were able to slow down and safely enjoy the view. Although we had seen most of the city at breakneck speed, we'd been enchanted by Medellin, "The City of Eternal Spring." Huge tropical flowers bloomed everywhere against a backdrop of lush green mountains. How could we not be impressed? Juan Valdez had not done his country justice. Medellin was far more beautiful than I ever imagined.

Pablo always carried his cell phone, and as we cruised the neighborhood, I said, "Pablo, can I borrow your phone?"

"Sure Ben, but why?"

"I want to call Nancy and tell her, 'Sell the house… We're moving to Medellin!'"

Pablo laughed. "She's going to think you've been buying drugs down here if you tell her that!"

We reached the airport far too soon and said farewell to Pablo. As we settled into our flight, I felt that bittersweet sensation once again of saying goodbye to a place I hadn't even wanted to visit but now had grown to love. Mike Fleetwood turned to me and smiled. "Well, Ben, I guess the only thing we needed to fear on this trip was losing our hearts to the Colombian people."

I smiled back. "I couldn't have said it better myself!"

Date: December 1997
Location: In Flight
Event: Writing in My Journal

JOURNAL NOTES & QUOTES

The country I had grown to love was falling away below me at a rate of a thousand feet per minute. I pulled out my journal to capture my impressions while they were still fresh and began to write…

Colombian memories which will be forever etched into my mind:

1. Running the gauntlet at the Medellin airport through an imaginary mob of "thugs, kidnappers, and mean and nasty bad men."
2. Scouting out Medellin, the former city of the Colombian drug king, Pablo Escobar.
   - North Medellin—Lunch at "The Old Hacienda"
   - Central Medellin—As we traveled through the city viewing historical sites, in broad daylight, we saw a 'Coke' processing plant where they were preparing

yet another shipment of the popular substance for unsuspecting youth. The shipment was so large they needed forklifts to move it—Coca-Cola not cocaine!

- *South Medellin—We traveled up steep mountain slopes known as 'Castilla,' where the poorer Colombians live in houses stacked one on top of the other. Stories of robbery, rape, and starvation still linger in my mind.*

3. *Most of all, I was impressed with the quality and professionalism of Pablo and his staff. He has an outstanding plan to reach Medellin, and I believe he will accomplish his plan!*

SPECIAL QUOTES:

Jacob Manthei	"Mom, you don't understand. There is no place safer than in the center of God's will!"
Mike Fleetwood	"Here's a Spanish lesson for running the gauntlet... 'Por favor, no blammo, no blammo!' which means 'Please, don't shoot! Don't shoot!'"
Pablo Cano	"This is an extraordinary time of opportunity, and we anticipate God moving in a mighty way as we partner together in the future."
Layo Leiva	"There is hope for Medellin!"

Our joint prayer together concluding the briefing:

"We look forward with great anticipation to meeting thousands of Colombians from this great harvest at that final banquet in heaven."

CONCLUSION:

What a great privilege to participate in what God is doing in Colombia! This trip will add great purpose to our God-given calling as businessmen. I will add Pablo and his staff to my daily prayer list. God is doing great things in Colombia!

4TH ASSIGNMENT— Continued

Special Agent Ben's Return to Colombia

Your assignment, should you choose to accept it, is to return to Colombia and use your expertise as a businessman in such a way as to inspire other businessmen to use their own L.I.F.E. to achieve true success and significance.

Your will speak on your 4 Keys to Personal Success and Tom will speak on 2 Qualities of Leadership that Money Can't Buy.

Pablo Cano will host your visit.

Mike Fleetwood will serve as your liaison and Layo Leiva will be your interpreter.

Date: October 1998
Location: The Office
Event: A Telephone Conversation

YOU WANT ME TO SPEAK IN COLOMBIA?

If they ask, I will go.

Immediately upon returning to the States, I had added the Businessmen's Seminar in Colombia to my list of things to pray about on my Prayer Walk. Through our finances, we already had provided the funds for Pablo to launch his new initiatives. But more importantly, I had been praying about his challenge to return. Whenever you brainstorm and cook up an idea, you're never quite sure if the other party will follow through on it or if they're just being polite. I decided between the Lord and me that if they asked me to come, I would go.

On this particular day I had already made three big blunders, and I was sitting in my office hoping to make it until five o'clock without another major mistake, when the phone buzzed, and I picked it up.

"Ben, you have a call on Line 3."

I wanted to say, "Take a message." Instead, for some reason I asked, "Who is it?"

"It's Mike Fleetwood from Campus Crusade for Christ International."

"Thanks, I'll take the call."

After the preliminary chit-chat, Mike said: "Ben, Pablo called to say they're working on the businessmen's seminar, and he wondered if you would still consider speaking. He would like you to use your *expertise* as a businessman to influence other businessmen for Christ."

The timing was so ironic in light of all the mistakes I had made that day. Then I remembered the morning in Colombia when Mike and I arrived at breakfast, looked at each other, and burst out laughing. Both of us had buttoned our shirts with one button off.

"Expertise? Mike, you've traveled with me. I can't believe you're asking me this! You want me to use my 'expertise?' I can't even button my shirt properly!"

Then I remembered my agreement with the Lord: *If they ask, I will go!*

I said, "I can't speak for the others, but you can tell Pablo I'd love to come and offer my encouragement."

Mike said, "I've already spoken with Tom and he's coming. But Ben, this is more than just offering encouragement. On Thursday night, you will be the *keynote speaker.* On Friday night, Tom will give the keynote address."

"Keynote speaker? What will I say?"

"You and Tom talk it over. I'm sure God will guide you. Think about what makes you tick. What are your keys to success? As soon as you get back to me with your topics, Pablo will print a brochure to send to all the businessmen in Medellin."

As I hung up the phone, I shook my head in disbelief. "You certainly have a sense of humor, don't you, Lord?" My day had been filled with defeat, yet here I was given the opportunity to use my business *expertise* as a platform to share Biblical keys to success with the entire business community of Medellin. Amazing!

Date: October 1998
Location: Corporate Offices
Event: A Conference Call

TOTAL SUCCESS 4X2

What a unique name! The seminar was billed as *Total Success 4x2* because I had four points and Tom had two.

We were not professional conference speakers by any stretch of the imagination. In fact, this was a first for us. We brainstormed together and decided I would speak on the micro-aspect of business, sharing the four daily disciplines to which I attribute my *personal* success. Tom would address the question: "To what do we attribute our *business* success?" He would explain the macro-aspect of business, sharing how we run our businesses with integrity and teamwork.

In October, we flew to Colombia and Pablo oriented us to the format of the conference. My talk on Thursday was entitled *My Competitive Advantage: Four Keys to Success*. Tom's Friday talk was listed as *Two Qualities of Leadership that Money Can't Buy*. Saturday's question/answer time was entitled *Achieving True Significance*.

A staff member would introduce us, and we would end our talks by telling the businessmen how they could each develop a personal relationship with the living God of the Universe. The true purpose of the seminar was to introduce people to Jesus. As American businessmen, we were simply the magnets to attract them by sharing truths they *wanted* to hear. They would then receive an added bonus—the truth they *needed* to hear.

Pablo explained that some of the men who had registered for the conference had refused to step foot in a church but were eager to learn about success from the perspective of an American businessman. He expected 250 businessmen at the sessions and 650 at the Saturday rally.

Have you ever felt honored and humbled at the same time? Just because we were *American businessmen,* we had a platform to speak in Colombia. We were no better or smarter than Colombian businessmen! We were simply Americans who had achieved success and were willing to share the principles we had learned about doing business God's way. What a privilege!

```
Date: Thursday, October 1998
Location: Medellin Conference Center
Event: Businessmen's Seminar
```

MY COMPETITIVE ADVANTAGE: FOUR KEYS TO SUCCESS

Talk about butterflies in my stomach!

Pablo's team had rushed us downtown to a high-rise building, parked in the underground ramp, and hustled us into the elevator. Our bodyguard led us into the conference room, which was set up to seat 300 attendees. Once we began to relax, Pablo led us outside onto a balcony that overlooked the sparkling lights of the city. I was just leaning over the rail to look down onto the street when, suddenly, I heard gunshots below us on the street.

I jumped back against the wall. *The drug lords are trying to kill me!*

Pablo saw the terror in my eyes and said, "No problema, Ben. No problema. Just firecrackers."

It took me five minutes to calm down until all I felt was butterflies again. Had I known that tomorrow's paper would confirm that people had indeed been murdered, I may never have been able to speak. When I had regained my composure, Pablo led me into the conference room where hundreds of businessmen were taking their seats.

I looked at Tom. "I wish you were speaking first. If nobody comes back tomorrow, it will be because I bombed out tonight. Then they won't get to hear your talk, and yours is the really important stuff."

Tom shook his head. "You'll do fine, Ben."

A minute later I turned to Mike. "I can't do this. You speak for me."

Mike said, "Oh Ben, just tell them...."

I'd done my homework and knew exactly what to say, but how do you prepare for the jitterbugs?

I sat down while Pablo addressed the crowd in Spanish, welcoming the men and introducing the seminar. Meanwhile, I rehearsed the theme of my talk: *"Where do you go when the pressure is on?"* Suddenly it struck me. The pressure was on! That's exactly what was happening, and I just needed to practice what I was about to preach.

When it was my turn to speak, Layo took his place in front of the microphone to interpret. I stood next to him and drew from his confidence. He translated so well that the men leaned forward and hung on every word.

My animated speech began with this:

"The score was tied. It was the NBA finals, there were five seconds remaining on the clock, and Larry Bird was at the free-throw line. The noisy crowd grew hushed. Every eye was fixed on this player who was about to determine the outcome of the biggest game of the year.

"Each free throw was executed perfectly, and the crowd exploded! It was a moment to remember. But what I found even more phenomenal was the TV interview afterward. They said, 'Larry, with all that pressure, thinking of the millions of people watching you and the prestige of winning the national championship and the money you might win, how could you focus and hit those free throws with all that on your mind?'

"Larry said, 'Simple. I wasn't thinking about any of that stuff! I was telling myself to "hold your elbow in, snap your wrist, follow through…" That's what was on my mind! I had done it so many times in preparation, it was just natural to me. You see, shooting free throws is one of my daily disciplines. Each day after practice, when the other guys hit the showers, I stay and shoot free throws.'

"When you find yourself under pressure and the heat is on during a big negotiation, what's on your mind? Are you thinking about the financial outcome or the status of the person you are dealing with? Or do you focus on the wisdom you have gained through your daily disciplines?

"A wise man once said, 'An all-star does every day what an average person does occasionally.'

"Every successful person I have met has developed specific daily disciplines to which they attribute their success. Tonight, I would like to share with you the daily disciplines I have learned from others, adopted as my own, and to which I attribute my personal success in business and in life.

#1 **I Read**

"When I get up in the morning, I spend fifteen minutes with the wisest man who ever lived. King Solomon wrote a little book in the Bible called Proverbs. The book has 31 chapters and, since most months have 31 days, I turn to the chapter that corresponds to that day of the month. That's where I get my wisdom for the day.

#2 **I Walk**

"Before I go to work, I take a walk and pray through the Lord's Prayer, applying each section to the events of my day. It's called "Prayer Walking." That's when I work on my relationships: first with God, second with my wife and kids, and then with my relationships at work. A big part of business is relationships. We've all experienced business meetings where someone comes with a chip on their shoulder, and it colors the whole meeting. Each of us has a positive or negative potential and we need to get our attitude straight for the day. So, on my daily walk, I pray about my relationships.

#3 **I Work**

"The third thing I do is work. Work is a prime place to test out the wisdom and relationship-builders we learned in steps #1 and #2. Last summer, we were awarded the largest job in the history of our company. We weren't the low bidder, nor were we the most qualified to do the work, but we won the job because we had built a reputation for doing quality work and honoring our commitments! Through our work, we had built a reputation for honesty and integrity that paid off. Work is also where I focus my energy into providing financial freedom for my family and gaining the resources to achieve my life goals in helping to fulfill the Great Commission.

#4 **I Listen**

"This is where I discover my life's purpose. At the end of the day, I sit in my hot tub and evaluate the day with an open heart to hear what God is trying to teach me. We often rush through life so fast that we miss this important step. If we do learn the lesson, it often stays in our heads but doesn't reach down into our hearts and lives. It takes time to process things and ask, 'How will this lesson affect my life? What do I need to change in my life as a result of what I learned today?' It takes even more time to listen for the answer. But it's time well spent. That's where I've developed real meaning and direction in my life.

"I've spent the past twenty years striving to build up my business and family. Now as I gaze at the world map hanging on the wall of the hot tub room, I think about ways I can spend the next twenty years building up God's business for eternity. That's when my life gains true vision and purpose as I work on my eternal business plan. We are all striving for true significance in life. How much more significant can your life be than to impact the lives of others in a positive way for all of eternity?

"May I encourage you to join God's team in reaching the world with the message of Jesus. When the Lord returns, may he find us involved in the battle and not on the sidelines watching."

With each point, I gained more confidence. By the time I had finished and taken my seat, the butterflies were forgotten, and I was totally energized because I had succeeded in doing my part.

After Pablo explained how to experience forgiveness for your sins and new purpose in life by receiving Jesus, I was surprised when several men approached me to ask if they could meet with me personally the next day. One, who owned a large furniture factory in Colombia, seemed especially anxious to meet with me in the morning.

Like Larry Bird at the free-throw line, my evening began with anxiety and pressure, but as I focused on the four disciplines God had built into my life, the results were outstanding.

```
Date: Friday morning
Location: Hotel Lobby
Event: A private meeting
```

A HEART IS CHANGED

The man not only showed up but brought two of his children!

This man was a distant relative of one of the Campus Crusade staff members, and she had prayed for his salvation for thirty years! His heart had been ice-cold toward Christianity all those years, and the only reason he had come to the seminar was to hear about "business success." However, when he heard how much God loves him and cares about how he runs his furniture business, it touched him deeply.

He was all smiles as we shook hands in greeting.

"Would you tell my two children what you told me last night? I brought them along so they could hear what you shared with me."

I told them about my four daily disciplines and challenged them to get involved in one of the Crusade churches. I rejoiced when they promised to attend the Saturday rally the next day. What a joy to be a tool in God's hand!

The second man who had scheduled an appointment with me was experiencing difficulties in his work as a soccer player. We talked about my trips to El Salvador with the basketball team, and I challenged him to begin Prayer Walking. He promised to run and pray through the Lord's Prayer each morning in Medellin while I walked and prayed each morning in Michigan. I promised to hang his picture in my hot tub room so I would remember to pray for him. I now have a counterpart in Medellin who is Prayer Walking with me.

I learned later that the Chief Financial Officer of the largest utility company in Colombia had attended the seminar and had prayed to receive Christ after the final gospel presentation concluded the meeting. With tears in his eyes, he had told a staff member that it was as if each of my four points was tailor-made for him.

What an incredible honor! I was so glad that I had said "yes" to God when I was asked to come to Colombia and, like Forrest Gump in the right place at the right time, I had positioned myself to see God's mighty and loving hand at work in these lives.

This experience was a powerful encouragement to me, reinforcing that we were on the right track in Colombia. God's Word does not return to Him void. It impacts the hearts and lives of people—for all eternity!

Special Agent: Tom
Date: Friday night
Location: Medellin Conference Center
Event: Businessmen's Seminar

TWO QUALITIES OF LEADERSHIP THAT MONEY CAN'T BUY

This is Ben's cousin Tom again, and it was my night to speak.

Ben and I are very different people. His style is personal and relational, so he spoke to the hearts of the businessmen. I have a more intellectual style that speaks to the mind. That's what makes us such a great team. Together, we are able to reach very different people, and I was excited about those I would share with tonight.

I began by answering a question.

◆ ◆ ◆

"Some of you might be wondering: 'What made you Americans want to come to Colombia?' Just in case you're asking, I'd like to get that question out of the way right off the bat. We're here because we want to get to know your culture. We want to share in the work of our friends from Campus Crusade for Christ International. And most importantly, we're here because of a covenant that God made with Abraham thousands of years ago! God said that He was going to bless Abraham's descendants and that they should become a blessing to every family on earth. As Christians, we are spiritual children of Abraham, and it is our duty to be a blessing not just to people in our own culture but to people from every culture. We are not here randomly, but we have come because God Himself commissioned us to go into all the world and share the blessings He has given us.

"I am here to encourage you as the business community in Colombia to become more than just successful business owners and leaders. I didn't risk my life and fly down here just to teach you how to make money. True success in life is about more than just money. I want to teach you to build biblical principles into your life that are far more valuable than money.

"When I was preparing this talk to share with you, I asked myself, 'What are the most important elements that make our business successful?'

"I could talk about a lot of different things. The physical ramifications of our business are this: I run a wood veneer mill with 150 employees. We make high quality veneer. Doing that requires several components.

- **We need a highly trained labor force**; therefore, we consider our employees our #1 asset!
- **We need to maintain consistent quality veneer and**

- **still stay competitive**; therefore, we utilize the most sophisticated technology available.
- **We need to know our niche market**; therefore, we have evaluated who we are and have worked hard to establish an integrated market plan.

"However, I am not going to talk to you about those issues today. Instead, I'm going to talk with you about two key elements in our businesses which money cannot buy: *Teamwork* and *Integrity*.

"*Integrity* is defined as 'a rigid adherence to a code of values.' Integrity begins by choosing a set of values that you believe in, then making your decisions based on those values no matter what the cost or circumstances. Because we are Christians, we choose to embrace the values of the Bible and apply those to our lives and businesses. The Bible says that 'A good name is more to be desired than silver or gold' (Proverbs 22:1), so we made it our first priority to develop a good name.

"To give you an example of how this works, I'd like to share a story with you about how we applied the principle of integrity to our business and how it contributed to our success.

"We had been cutting wood for a company in Korea and were very surprised one day to receive a notice from them informing us that they were rejecting seventeen container-loads of our wood. We're talking hundreds of thousands of dollars' worth of veneer. They had changed the grade of wood on the order, and we didn't receive the change order until after we had seventeen loads in the pipeline. Since the loads were paid for in advance by letter of credit, we had no obligation to pay for the error. We had a strong legal case that could prove this was their mistake. However, we agonized over the situation because we were committed to integrity in our business dealings.

"Finally, I called our management team together and asked everyone to help in the problem-solving process. I told the team, 'It is not an option for us to keep the money and call it their problem. That would destroy our relationship with the Korean company. I'd like you to think about how we might solve this problem, and we'll meet again in a few days.'

"At our next meeting, the team came up with a strategy and contacted the Korean company to tell them our plan. We agree to replace all seventeen loads with this stipulation. Each time you order three new loads, we will send you one free replacement load in the shipment.

"The solution benefited us because it guaranteed continued business with their company. At the same time, it benefited the Koreans who got their wood replaced with the proper grade for free. They were thrilled because they hadn't expected us to pay for their mistake, and they became loyal customers after that. They got all that wood replaced for free, and we maintained a long-term relationship. Everyone came out a winner.

"When we applied the principle of integrity, we earned a good name which was far more valuable than the silver or gold we lost in those seventeen loads. We built a relationship of trust that brought us continued business for several years.

"As in this story, integrity requires tremendous creativity, which leads me to the next point. It was not until we brought in our management team that we solved the problem. Therefore, the second essential element to which I attribute our business success is *Teamwork*. One definition of a team is: 'Any group organized to work together.' Teamwork is the backbone of our business success.

"*Teamwork is the fuel that allows common people to achieve uncommon results.* If each team member brings his strengths to bear on a subject, you can overcome almost any obstacle. That's how we came up with our solution to the Korean situation.

"My personal definition of teamwork is: 'People contributing their own strong points while covering the other member's weak points.' Covering a weak point doesn't mean ignoring it, but rather making provision for the weakness. You have to understand your teammate's weakness and then make provision to cover it with your strength. If one person is not good at math and you are, then you provide the math component. If the other is good at English and contributes that component, then you have both Math and English covered.

"Human nature tends to do just the opposite. When you see someone else with a weak point, it's easy to point out that weak point and forget that this is an opportunity to contribute your own strong point to the team.

"Have you ever heard the story of 'The Pecking Chickens?' When our family raised chickens, I noticed one day that a chicken had lost a few feathers. Pretty soon, another chicken came by and pecked at the bare spot on its back. I didn't think much about it until a second chicken came along and took another peck and a spot of blood appeared. Then another chicken came by to peck at it and pretty soon the bleeding chicken was surrounded by others who took turns pecking and pecking until they literally pecked the chicken to death!

"We humans tend to do the same thing. When we see a weak point in a teammate, if we spend our time picking on them and ridiculing them, we have no energy to contribute our own strong point. The team breaks down and everybody loses.

"Teamwork requires us to make two choices. First, we must choose to contribute our own strong points. Second, we choose to cover the other person's weak points. These steps provide the fuel that allows common people like us to accomplish uncommon goals. That's what allows an average company to compete with anybody in the world and become successful.

"I'd like to tell you the story of the lion and the gazelle. Every morning in Africa, a gazelle wakes up and knows that it must run faster than the fastest lion or it will be eaten. And every morning a lion also wakes up and knows that it must run faster than the slowest gazelle or it will starve to death. It doesn't matter if you're a lion or a gazelle. When you wake up in the morning, you'd better be running! Both animals can survive, but they have to work to their peak level of performance. The same principle holds true in business. In order to survive and compete, you need to know who you are. Are you a lion or a gazelle?

"If you're a small company, don't try to compete with a big, international company. If you go head-to-head with them, they will beat you every time. You need to discover your own niche market. If you're the big company and you try to work your way into all the little niche markets, your overhead will kill you. Therefore, you must evaluate who you are and put your team together in a way that will take advantage of your particular mix.

"I'd like to challenge you to explore these two concepts of *Teamwork* **and** *Integrity*. If you do, I think you will find that you can build a business that is both rewarding and biblical in style, and which will enable God to bless your business.

"However, if you choose to violate God's principles, His character prevents Him from blessing you. God is not required to bless your business just because you might call yourself a Christian. You need to apply His principles to your businesses if you want God to bless the efforts of your hands.

"In conclusion, our family has found that in order to make our businesses successful, we need to develop teams of professional people who will choose to contribute their strong points while covering the other's weak points. We also need to apply the principle of integrity to every situation. After that, the principles of labor force, technology, and niche markets fall into place beautifully.

"I'd like to thank you for your attention and if you have any questions, I'd be happy to chat with you personally or field your questions tomorrow during the designated time…"

◆ ◆ ◆

The room burst into a round of applause and Pablo ended the evening with warm concluding remarks and an invitation to the Saturday Pep Rally. Thus ended the businessmen's seminar and we heard afterward that everyone felt they had gotten their money's worth.

As we debriefed that night, Ben and I felt very privileged to be a part of God's plan to bring "Total Success" to Pablo's ministry and into the lives of many businessmen in Medellin, Colombia.

Date: Saturday, October 1998
Location: Auditorium in Medellin
Event: Pep Rally

PEP RALLY 101

The atmosphere was charged with excitement. The roar of the crowd filled the gymnasium as people jumped to their feet, screaming and cheering while waving colorful flags.

Was this the championship basketball series? No, but it certainly felt like it. There was no ball and there were no jerseys. Instead, every person was a player—from leaders to newcomers—they were all celebrating what God had done through their team that month in the city of Medellin.

Pablo's ministry had 16 house churches when we met at The Old Hacienda to discuss strategy. Now, ten months later, the number had grown to 28! Pablo was well on his way to reaching his goal of 50 churches throughout Medellin. Scattered throughout the city, the congregations met individually each week and came together once a month for a pep rally to celebrate.

I looked at the 650 faces assembled and marveled at how different this church service was from any I had experienced back home. When Pablo introduced the first group, they screamed and waved flags and chanted their slogan. Each section had its own slogan and colorful flags, and each church yelled louder than the last!

After delivering a motivating message from the Bible, Pablo turned on the overhead projector. "These were our goals for last month. Let me show you what God did!" His update on each church was punctuated with enthusiastic applause. As soon as he had finished one report, he began another. "Here are our goals for the next month." One church had scheduled a neighborhood party, another was visiting door-to-door. It took half an hour to explain the specific plans of each congregation.

When Pablo finished his report, he joined Tom and I for the time of singing, and I asked, "Do you do that every month when you get together?"

He nodded. "I have to! If they couldn't rejoice over our progress toward reaching Medellin, and if I didn't impart the vision for where we are headed in the future, the people would lose momentum. The Bible says, 'Without a vision, the people perish!' (Proverbs 29:18). If we weren't diligent to keep their attention focused on forward motion, they would turn inward, only thinking of their own group. Each month they need a fresh sense of their own integral part in a movement that is reaching their city for Christ."

I loved being with these Latinos. They were so full of life, and as music flooded the auditorium, they threw themselves into worship with gusto. When the music ended, it was time for our segment of the rally where we could answer questions from the conference. We walked to the podium and Claudia interviewed us.

"Tom, how would you define true significance?"

Tom said, "True significance is using your God-given abilities for eternal purposes." He then explained how we applied that principle to our businesses.

Then Claudia turned to me. "Is it possible to give if you don't have money?"

I laid out the L.I.F.E. principle, placing special emphasis on Labor, Influence, and Expertise. I learned afterward that my response was a big hit with those folks who were struggling financially. Several people came up to me and said, "I never thought about it before, but I have a lot to give!"

Then Claudia asked, "What is your most outstanding memory of the Colombian people?"

I said, "How crazy Manuel drives!" I pointed to my temple and drew circles with my finger. "Muy loco!" (Very crazy!)

The crowd went wild! I had spoken in Spanish and poked fun at one of their own. People laughed and pointed at Manuel. "Muy loco! Muy loco!" It was great fun.

When Claudia finished her questions, Pablo asked the three of us Americans to stand next to him. What's this all about? I wondered. He reached under the podium, pulled out three colorful ponchos and said: "Put them on! Put them on!" Our interpreter explained that Pablo had just made us honorary PAYSA's (native Colombians). For us, it was like being inducted into a native American tribe, like the Cherokees. What an honor!

When the meeting ended, the man from the furniture company thanked me for inviting him and said he was deeply moved by the meeting. This was the first church experience of his life and what an introduction. It was exciting—there was passion, cheering, action, enthusiasm, vision, and accomplishments. What could be more motivating to a successful businessman? Once again, it was as though God had tailor-made a message just for him.

He then introduced me to the rest of his family. "Ben, would you tell my wife and other children what you shared with me that first night?"

"Of course." I grinned and thought: *This is what life is all about!* I couldn't imagine any greater joy.

What a pep rally!

ASSIGNMENT DEBRIEFED

EXPERTISE? Some days I feel like I can't even button my shirt right. Yet the truth is that each of us has been given unique gifts and talents. What are yours?

Through this assignment I learned that despite my own feelings of inadequacy, **I do have areas of Expertise!** God is not looking for perfect people but for willing hearts. He is able to transform our humble service into mighty deeds, as when He used my expertise as a businessman to impact one man whose heart had been hardened to every other messenger. What an exciting privilege to be on God's team!

During my weekend of turmoil over whether or not to travel to Colombia, I was forced to evaluate my faith at a much deeper level. Did I believe God's Word enough to risk my life? This struggle tested my character and allowed me to see exactly what was in my heart. Eventually, God's Spirit won out and enabled me to embrace the principle: **Obedience is more important than safety.**

As with each assignment, I came home convinced that **we would have missed such a blessing** if we had stayed home where it was "safe." I fell in love with the people and the country of Colombia.

Is God prompting you to use *your expertise* in a way that stretches you beyond your comfort zone? Do you have something to share that you never really thought about before?

PEP RALLY 101 | 249

Ben's Fears of "Running the Gauntlet" at the Colombia Airport

THE NEXT ASSIGNMENT

Special Agent 'You' Assignment to the World

Your assignment, should you choose to accept it, is to go wherever God leads you and use your L.I.F.E. to share the love of Jesus and to touch the souls of people for eternity.

You will be escorted by friends you may not know yet as you are led by the Living God of the Universe.

THE L.I.F.E. OF A SPECIAL AGENT

Special Agent 'You':
Assignment to the World

```
Date: Now
Location: Your Prayer Walk
Event: Your Business Plan
```

HOW TO DEVELOP YOUR ETERNAL BUSINESS PLAN

So how about you? Have you decided to pursue deeper significance in your life? Are you looking for ways to use your L.I.F.E. to have an impact on others for all eternity?

If so, you may be asking: "Where do I begin? What is my next assignment?" A wise man once said, "You can only give as much as you've received." All I can offer you are a few steps that have worked for me. You may come up with better ideas yourself.

First, pray! I asked God to help me understand the difference between success and significance and show me how to invest my L.I.F.E. for eternal dividends. I asked Him to provide opportunities to enlarge my territory and give me the courage to say, "Yes" when those opportunities presented themselves. Then I opened my heart to hear His prompting, which positioned me to see His mighty hand at work.

Second, do your homework! You can be active while you wait for your assignment. For a more in-depth understanding of how to use your life for eternal significance, I recommend Kent R. Hunter's book, *Life Beyond Ordinary: Investing Your Life for Eternal Significance.* You can also evaluate your life and ask, 'What is my own particular mix of gifts? What do I have to offer?' Then, you can investigate different ministries to discover which ones might fit your mix of giftings. Go online and register to let them know what you have to offer. *(See Appendix E: Register Here.)* Who knows where it might lead? Only the Master knows what kind of adventure will fulfill your deepest longings and yield the greatest results for His Kingdom.

Third, be ready to say "Yes!" I discovered that the key to true significance is found in being obedient to God's quiet prompting in your heart! It means acting upon what God is leading you to do and using your success to make a difference in a way that will impact people's lives a thousand years from now. This brings extreme fulfillment and purpose in life. Try it!

I can guarantee you'll like it.

Fourth, Go! Let the adventure begin!

```
Special Agent: Nancy
Date: September 2000
Location: Home
Event: Weighing It Up!
```

PROS & CONS OF OVERSEAS MISSIONS

I'd like to introduce you to my wife, Nancy. She's short, cute, bubbly, and boy can she cook! She has the same gift of hospitality as my mother. But the thing I've grown to treasure most about Nancy through our many years of marriage is her open-hearted relationship with our children. They can tell her anything, knowing she will understand. I couldn't have asked for a better role model for the next generation. I hope you catch a glimpse of her heart as you read her story.

◆ ◆ ◆

Hi! Ben asked me to share with you how things look from a wife's perspective. To be honest with you, it took me some time to weigh up the pros and cons of our new L.I.F.E. adventure.

I struggled when Ben went on his first mission trip. It wasn't fun waiting at home while he traveled into remote regions in Mongolia. Our son, Andy, was very young and very sick. It was challenging to take care of him and run the household alone. Things started to go wrong as soon as Ben left. The furnace quit working, the transmission went out in the car, and we had a huge snake in the basement! All the while, I worried about what might be happening to Ben on his journey.

Ben and I talked things over when he came home, and we wondered if this idea of getting involved personally with a missionary endeavor was really worth the effort, especially when I heard about his hair-raising flights on Mongolia's domestic airlines.

But then I saw the eyes of our children sparkle with delight as they listened to Ben's stories, and I watched them grow excited about something beyond themselves. Their world expanded as we prayed for the mayor of Uliastai and the people of Mongolia. More importantly, their hearts grew too.

I decided that the benefits strongly outweighed the sacrifices because Ben's involvement had such a positive effect on our children.

Several years ago, our family traveled to the interior of Jamaica where people still wash their clothes in the river. I had never seen such poverty. Our children were not afraid of roughing it or getting dirty. In fact, they viewed it as an exciting adventure, just like their dad had experienced. Later, Lindsey went back to Jamaica with her youth group and Jacob went to China with Ben. Their own mission experiences taught them to appreciate how good they have it here at home. They don't take things for granted anymore, like hot showers, bathrooms, and a closet full of clothes. They're much less selfish now that they understand how blessed they truly are!

Personally, I struggle when going into places of extreme suffering. When we visited the orphanage in Jamaica, I cried the whole time. My heart broke too much to help. But I love it when people like Hogan come to stay at our house. I can invest my Labor and Expertise into entertaining them and I feel very comfortable using my gifts in that capacity. Of course, my greatest joy is to invest my entire L.I.F.E. every day into the souls of our three children and to watch them grow into the amazing people God created them to be. That is *my* most incredible adventure!

Over the years, I've grown much better at supporting Ben in his travels. It's never easy to let him go. Something bad could happen to him. But something could happen to him here too. So, I pray for him and keep the flight tracker going on my computer when he travels. I know exactly where he is at all times and feel very much a part of what he's doing. I'm still not thrilled when Ben goes into dangerous places, but we've decided that unless we are both in full agreement, he will not go. Nine times out of ten, he has my full support.

When Ben comes home from a mission trip, he is always so energized. It's great fun to hear his stories and watch the children enter into his excitement.

Is it worth it? Absolutely! I wouldn't trade this L.I.F.E. for anything!

Date: Any Time
Location: Your Life
Event: True Significance

WHAT CAN YOU EXPECT?

Is it really worth all the effort? How might your L.I.F.E. change?

I discovered that the key to developing true significance is found in being obedient to God's quiet prompting in my heart. When I act upon what God is leading me to do and use my success to make a difference in a way that will impact lives a thousand years from now, this brings extreme fulfillment and purpose in life.

When I sit in my hot tub at the end of the day, when my responsibilities are fulfilled and my mind is free to drift off, I gaze at the world map on my wall and wonder: *What does God have in store for me to do next to impact the world in a positive way for eternity through my L.I.F.E.? Where might my next assignment take me?* Even as I contemplate new prospects or problems in our business, I do so in light of my L.I.F.E.'s purpose. That's my passion. I can't imagine a more fulfilling way to spend the rest of my life. *(See Appendix C: Favorite Quotes.)*

We live in a thrilling time in history. Of all the people who ever lived on the face of the earth, how many of them do you think are living today? Ten percent? Actually, as of 2002, over *half* of the people that had ever lived in the history of the world were alive and walking the planet. Just think what the number is now! I used to think it must have been so exciting to be a disciple at the time of Christ when the early church was turning their world upside down. But the opportunity set before us today is even more staggering. We have the potential of impacting the lives of over half the people who have ever lived. What an exciting time!

I learned three new principles as I began to use my L.I.F.E. toward eternal significance.

First, you cannot steer a ship unless it is moving. Unless we are willing to be obedient to get started, how can God steer us to do future things? God is not able to take us to the next level until we are obedient to do what He has already shown us. I remember times in my life when I was not obedient and found my life stagnating without knowing why. I'm glad those days are over, and I hope I never go there again.

Second, for every door we walked through, God opened two more! When we were obedient to visit China on a visionary trip, God opened two more doors by providing an opportunity to visit Wanzhou City, and then later to return with the Rag-Tag Team. When I was obedient when asked to use my influence as a businessman to speak to military leaders in Russia, God opened two more doors by providing an opportunity to speak at the Businessmen's Seminar in Colombia and later to speak at a World Briefing in Cancun, Mexico.

Third, when you don't know what to do, do what you know. At one time I decided I wouldn't do anything until God spoke to me directly. That was faulty thinking. God has already shown us many things to do. We know we are to be kind, to pray for others, to help the widows and orphans, to visit those who are sick and in prison, and to make disciples in every nation. Our family discovered that until we were obedient to do those things that He had already made clear in Scripture, God did not open new doors. But once we began to do what we knew to do, He opened two more doors and gave us opportunities beyond our imagination.

I have been privileged to experience the adventure of allowing God to accomplish His goals through my L.I.F.E. and make a difference for eternity. That's what made the Colombia assignment so exciting to me. When I was obedient to go, despite the dangers, God accomplished His goal of salvation for an entire family which made a difference in their lives for all eternity.

I would like to leave you with this challenge: If you are obedient to do one thing you already know to do, God may open more exciting opportunities than you can even imagine. The sky's the limit.

```
Date: Once Upon a Time
Location: A Classroom
Event: A Lecture
```

TIME MANAGEMENT 101

Is it hard to imagine how you might fit anything else into your life? With all the pressures of work and family, do you have the time or energy to invest your L.I.F.E. for eternity? Is the present sometimes more than you can handle already?

I've felt that way many times. If you're asking yourself those kinds of questions, let me share with you the lessons I learned in "Time Management 101."

A professor stood at the podium and pulled out a wide-mouth jar. Then he reached under the podium, pulled out several rocks, and placed them into the jar. When he couldn't fit any more rocks into the jar, he asked, "How many of you think this jar is full?"

Many students raised their hands.

"Let's see if you're right," the professor said. He reached under the podium, pulled out a container of stone chips, and began pouring them into the jar. He shook the jar so the chips would fill the voids and continued pouring until no more stone chips would fit into the jar. Then he asked again, "How many of you think this jar is full?"

Someone said, "You might be able to fit a little more in."

The professor said, "You're right!" He reached under the podium and pulled out a cup of sand and poured it into the big jar. Then he asked one more time, "How many of you think this jar is full?"

We said, "No, you can probably fit something more into it."

The class was silent, and he reached down to pull out a cup of water. When the jar was filled to the brim, the professor asked a final question.

"What is the point of this lesson?"

One student raised his hand and said, "No matter how full you think your schedule is, you can probably fit in just a little more!"

The professor said, "That's not even close. **The point of this illustration is: If you want to fit the big rocks into the jar, you have to put them in first or you won't have room for them at all!**"

That is the lesson of Time Management 101. If you want to accomplish the most important things in your life, you'd better put them into your schedule first!

For me, the big rocks are the things I do that will continue to yield dividends a thousand years from now—the things that will make a difference for all eternity:

- The Godly character we build into our own life;
- The relationships we build with our spouse and our children;
- The souls of people in our lives, in our communities, and around the world;

- Being faithful in the profession God has called me into and using my L.I.F.E. success as a tool of God to accomplish His eternal purpose.

Those are the "big rocks" that I want to make sure I put into my schedule first, or they'll never fit in at all!

What are the big rocks in your life? Have you found a way to fit them into your schedule first? If your jar is already full, might it be possible to empty it and start over by putting in the big rocks first?

Date: A Lifetime
Location: Your Heart
Event: Giving to Others

WHY DO YOU GIVE?

Some people give out of guilt, some out of duty, and some give simply because they have a generous heart. How about you? Why do you give?

Over the years, my reasons for giving have changed. Each step was a significant part of my growth process.

#1   The first reason I gave was out of *training*.

> I grew up with the principle of giving. It was the key to which my father attributed his own success in life. When I was ten years old, my father decided it was time to teach me to run my first business. We lived in the country, so he bought me a cow, and my job was to milk the cow each day and sell the milk to the family. I made twenty dollars a month. Then he taught me to calculate 10% of my income and give it to our church. After I was paid, I dropped two dollars into the collection plate at church.
>
> One day the cow stepped in the bucket, and because this was my only income, I fought hard to save that pail

of milk. From that day on, I never drank milk because I saw what went into it when the cow stepped in the bucket. Finally, the day the cow died was one of the happiest days of my life. When I received my final paycheck, I was so grateful that I doubled my tithe and gave four dollars!

#2   The second reason I gave was out of *obedience* to God.

Psalm 67 speaks about the Triangle of Blessing and requires us to pass along the blessings we receive so that others can rejoice and give the praise back to God.

#3   The third reason I gave was a result of developing *personal relationships*. Back in 1993, my cousin Tim had challenged us to change the way we were giving.

Tim said, "We need to stop this passive approach of giving corporately out of our business. It's so impersonal. Each of us needs to give individually and get involved at a personal level, traveling with the missionaries of our choice, building relationships with their people, and getting involved directly in their lives."

At first, we said, "Tim, that's a crazy idea!" But the more we thought about it, the more we liked his active approach and deliberately began to look for ways to get involved. Little did we know how this seemingly minor change in perspective would impact our lives.

Tim's idea was the key that opened doors for us to add our Labor, Influence, and Expertise to what we were already giving through our Finances.

As a result of Tim's challenge, each of us partnered with projects that stirred our own hearts, and we began to travel with those missionaries to see how we might help them. We would report back to the family team when we returned so they could get excited about the different ways God was using our businesses. The whole concept of *Helping to Fulfill the Great Commission* moved from our heads into our hearts as we developed personal relationships with people in the countries to which we gave. It was exciting to see God's hand at work.

Once I built relationships with the leaders on my assignments, I invested in their ministries out of love for the people in their circle of influence.

#4   The fourth reason I gave was out of *purpose*.

As we began to team up with different ministries and become partners in reaching their goals, my own work took on a whole new meaning. This not only changed the reason I gave, but also the reason I worked. Now I both work and give as a significant member of a team that is touching lives for eternity.

#5   The fifth reason I now give is out of sheer *love* for Jesus.

As I continued to talk about my L.I.F.E. with the Lord on my Prayer Walks, and as our assignments positioned us to see the mighty hand of God at work, I found myself loving Jesus at a much deeper level. I now realize that *love* is the most significant reason to give, so I invest out of sheer love and appreciation for His tremendous heart for the world.

It took me years to learn these truths. If you can grab hold of them now, just think what an adventure your life can be. There's no limit to where God might take you. So, fasten your seat belt. You could be in for the ride of your life!

How about it? Are you ready to give?

```
Date: Today
Location: Wherever You Are
Event: Another Challenge
```

WHY DO YOU DO WHAT YOU DO?

How would you define your worldview? Are you familiar with the term? Or are you like I was—totally unaware that you even have a worldview? I was surprised to learn that my worldview dictates nearly everything I do.

Why does one person lavish himself with limousines, fancy vacations, and five condos in exotic places, while the next person gives up everything he has and goes to a foreign land to become a missionary? Why does one family invest their L.I.F.E. in reaching the world for Christ while another family seeks every pleasure the world has to offer here and now? Why such extremes?

The reason we do what we do is based on our worldview. Our worldview is simply the way we view the world. It is our particular set of values and beliefs. It determines what we will choose to do and how we will respond to life situations. Our worldview is the lens through which we view life. It helps us process events, set goals, organize time, and understand events. Our worldview determines how we see the world, how we go about living our lives, and what type of society and nation we will build.

I believe that it is only to the degree that an individual or society is able to reject false worldviews and adopt the worldview of the kingdom of God as revealed through the life of Jesus that he or she will be able to experience the life and freedom that God intends for us as His children.

We all live according to what we believe deep-down in our innermost being. That's why these questions are so important. How do you view the world? Do you believe there is a God? If so, is your god personal and loving or an impersonal force in the universe? Or is there no god at all? And what about humans? Are we basically good or evil or somewhere in between? What about the past? Where did we all come from? Why are we here? And what about the future? Is today all we have to live for? Or is there a heaven and a hell, and can we choose today where we would like to spend eternity? (*See Characteristics of Opposing Worldviews and the Great Disconnect.*)

Your worldview will determine how you live your L.I.F.E.! What is your worldview? Why do you do what you do?

Have you started with one "Worldview" and gone through the Great Disconnect ending with logical results from a different "Worldview?"

The Great Disconnect
STARTING WORLD VIEW

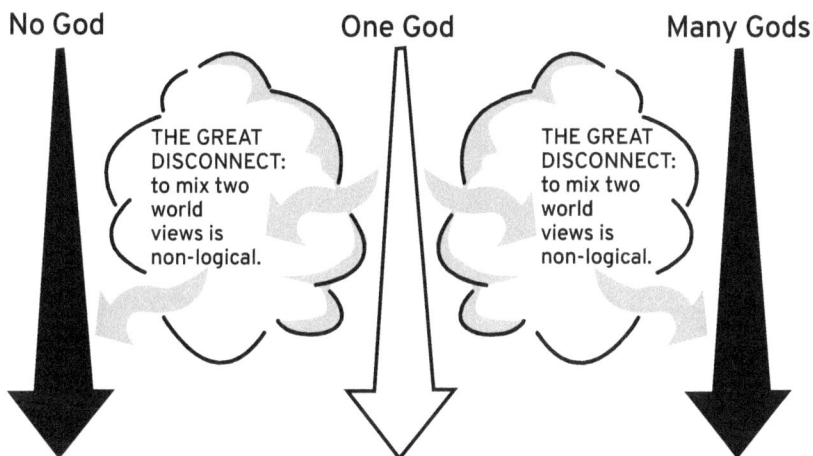

No God

LOGICAL RESULTS
- Evolution
- Euthanasia
- Abortion
- Survival of the Fittest

One God

LOGICAL RESULTS
- Blessings of Obedience (Heaven)
- Curses of Disobedience (Hell)
- Relationship Reconciled with God through Jesus

Many Gods

LOGICAL RESULTS
- Reincarnation Fatalism—the gods determine our fate
- New Age Movement Self-Awareness— we are all gods as discovered from within

THE GREAT DISCONNECT: to mix two world views is non-logical.

Date: Still Today
Location: Wherever You Are
Event: Some Serious Questions

THE GREAT DISCONNECT

Look at the Worldview Chart on the previous page. Are your beliefs consistent with one worldview? Or do they shift from one column to another?

If you are one of those people whose worldview is mixed, you're not alone! Many people begin with one particular worldview, but as they go through life accepting different opinions from various people, they pick and choose what they will believe and often end up with conclusions that belong to a different worldview than their own. If you were to trace a particular belief backwards to its logical origin, you may find that belief originated in a worldview that you would otherwise reject. This phenomenon is called the Great Disconnect.

For example, a Christian may believe in God and consider himself a follower of Jesus Christ yet believe in evolution because he is convinced that science proves it to be true. However, if you take a close look at the Worldview Chart, you will find that evolution is a belief that originates in naturalism, which states: "There is no God. There is no Creator."

CHARACTERISTICS OF OPPOSING WORLDVIEWS AND THE GREAT DISCONNECT

NATURALISM/ SECULARISM	THEISM	ANIMISM/ HUMANISM
No God	One God	Many gods; We are all gods
No spiritual reality	God created all things perfect and is actively involved	Spirits inhabit rocks, trees, water, etc.
Ultimate reality is found only in nature.	Ultimate reality found in a balance between physical and spiritual.	Ultimate reality found only in the spiritual.
Motto: Eat, drink, and be merry for tomorrow we die	Motto: Blessings for obedience, curses for disobedience. The choice is ours.	Motto: Fatalism: Our fate is predetermined by the gods OR We are all gods— We can build the ideal world
Life is a closed system, resources run out. We control our destiny.	Life is an open system. Knowledge is the ultimate renewable resource.	Questions if there really is a system.
Man dies. The End	Man's soul lives forever— Heaven or hell	Man is reborn— Reincarnation
Evolution, Atheism, and Secular Humanism find their roots in Naturalism.	Christianity, Judaism, and Islam find their roots in Theism.	The New Age Movement and Buddhism find their roots in Animism.
No Hope	Hope through Jesus	No Hope

If you have never looked at your own worldview or determined whether you have gone through the Great Disconnect, you might want to take some time to check into it. Truly, it will have a tremendous impact on the choices you make today and every day!

To gain a more complete understanding of the three world views and how they influence our nation, I recommend reading, *The Worldview of the Kingdom of God,* by Miller, Moffitt, and Allen. It explains this concept in terms that are easy to understand.

Why do you do what you do? Have you embraced one of the three major worldviews? Or are you a mixed bag? Is God prompting you to re-evaluate or make a change?

```
Date: The Future
Location: ???
Event: The End
```

FINISHING STRONG

How would you like to finish your life? What might you do today to help ensure that you will finish strong?

As I pondered these questions in my own life, I was reminded of an incident I had experienced with my son, Jake.

◆ ◆ ◆

I snuck a quick look over my shoulder and forced my feet to keep running. I couldn't believe what I was seeing. Jake was going to pass me! Jake and I were running up the final hill before our driveway, which was also the steepest incline on our route. Today was the first time I ever saw Jake get a sparkle in his eye, a kick in his step, and speed past me to the finish line. It made my day!

Just the day before, I had shared with Jake about two people in my life who had earned my deep respect by the way they finished strong.

I told Jake that my father went out in a blaze of color. He died in October when the trees were at their peak and his grave was covered with leaves of gold, which was so fitting for the way he finished strong. My father probably encouraged more people during his last two months of illness than in the preceding seventy years put together. He called people to ask for their forgiveness, to thank them for their presence in his life, and just to say goodbye. He not only taught us how to live; he also taught us how to die. He embraced the cancer as his "shortcut to heaven" and viewed our final days together as "a special time of visitation from the Lord." He went out like the trees of fall that build to their most vibrant colors just before the leaves drop off and they're done.

The second person I had told Jake about was Col. Coffman, an army colonel with a distinguished career. After he retired, he became a full-time missionary to the military men and women of Russia. During our trip to Russia, Col. Coffman challenged us with a reading from 2 Timothy 4:5-7, then summarized it with four points I will never forget.

1. Be cool.
2. Hang tough.
3. Be an evangelist.
4. Finish strong.

That's exactly how Col. Coffman lived. He finished strong and then went to his eternal reward.

I also read Jake a letter Hogan had sent after we returned from Mongolia.

Let me share a few things that are on my heart. Throughout this transitional period, I've experienced an unusual battle with our mutual enemy, Satan. Of all things, he's actually been congratulating me on my success, slapping me on the back, saying,

"Good job! From 6 to 500 on the ELIC team in ten years. Not bad. Nearly 2,000 teachers already sent and nearly 200,000 students touched by Christian love."

Then the stinger:

"Hey man, you're 52 years old. Give it a rest. Be content with all that's been accomplished. Slow down!"

How subtle. How dangerous. Drawing attention to what has already been done in Jesus' name—to distract me from the urgency of the work that remains."

Jake and I talked about Hogan's letter and his desire to keep up the pace in the battle and not peter out at the end.

Jake had been jogging with me to the lake and back for several days now, and even though at the time he was fifteen and I was forty-three, I always beat him back to the driveway. When we reached the final hill, I would give it a kick to run up the final stretch while Jake would slow down. But on this day, Jake went flying past me!

It made my day because I could see that Jake had not only listened to my stories about my father and Col. Coffman, but he had taken them to heart and kicked it in gear to finish strong.

◆ ◆ ◆

I have two goals I strive toward that will help me to finish strong. My first goal is to continue Prayer Walking—to walk with my Lord all the days of my life and then walk with Him into eternity. My second goal for finishing strong is to share with my children and those in my circle of influence how they can live their own L.I.F.E. in a way that will last for eternity. I strive to invest my energy today in a way that will continue beyond my own brief life. Someday, I hope to hear Jesus say, "Well done, good and faithful servant." That will truly be the most significant moment of my L.I.F.E.!

What are you doing today that will last beyond your lifetime? What goals might you strive toward that will enable you to finish strong?

Date: Anytime
Location: Wherever your story takes you
Event: Your Next Assignment

THE BOOK OF L.I.F.E

Have you ever imagined what it will feel like the day you arrive in heaven and hear your name read from the Lamb's Book of Life? That will be the most incredible day of all!

But could you imagine, in the meantime, encouraging a multitude of others by sharing your own incredible L.I.F.E. adventure as an improbable special agent in a book of L.I.F.E. down here?

Hebrews 10:24 says, "Let us consider how to stimulate one another unto love and good deeds."

Before you book your next travel package, consider combining your plans with a Special Agent L.I.F.E. Assignment. Your vacation can yield eternal dividends by teaming up with a missionary and sharing the very heartbeat of God.

Date:
Location:
Event:

MY SPECIAL AGENT L.I.F.E. JOURNAL

How I Became a Special Agent ....

....

....

....

My Eternal Business Plan ....

....

....

....

How I used my LABOR ....

....

....

....

....

....

How I used my INFLUENCE ....

....

....

....

....

....

How I used my FINANCES ....

....

....

....

....

....

How I used my EXPERTISE ....

....

....

....

....

....

How I encouraged others to use their L.I.F.E. for eternity. ....

....

....

....

....

....

FAVORITE QUOTES I heard along the way ....

....

....

....

....

How I Plan to Finish Strong

SQJ—STORIES, QUESTIONS, AND JOURNALING

S. **STORIES** *create a memorable way of learning new ideas through someone else's experience.*

Q. **QUESTIONS** *lead us to wrestle with new ideas and process what they really mean.*

J. **JOURNALING** *helps us imagine how those ideas might look in our own lives.*

S.Q.J. is the secret ingredient that propels learning from Informational to Transformational!

How have these stories inspired Transformation Learning in your life? Here are some questions to help trigger your thoughts.

CHAPTER 1: DECISIONS

- Despite his business successes, Ben said he knew deep inside that there was more to life than making money. Has there been a time in your life when you worried too much about making money and spent too much time working? How did that affect your family or other important relationships? Do you have any regrets about that time in your life?

- Ben's life was changed when he encountered a group of people who invested not only their money but their lives into endeavors with eternal significance. What do you think "endeavors with eternal significance" means? Give some examples of what would qualify as something that would have an eternal impact.

CHAPTER 2: SMOKING THE PEACE PIPE

- In Ben's family, supper always ended with Bible reading, prayer, and a hymn with mandatory attendance. Did you have family devotions growing up? Do you have family devotions now or any plans to? What do you see as the main challenges to consistently have devotions together as a family?

- After seeing firsthand how his formerly atheist roommate changed after receiving Christ, Ben realized that despite growing up in a Christian home, he hadn't made Christ the Lord and Master of his life. Is there an area of your life that you still want to control and where you haven't let Jesus be the Master?

CHAPTER 3: KICKING OFF THE SECOND HALF

- When Ben turned 40, he realized half of his life had already been lived. Twenty years from now, what do you want your life to look like?

- What needs to change in order for that to happen?

CHAPTER 4: PRAYER WALKING

- At a men's conference, the Holy Spirit challenged Ben with these questions: *How much time do I invest each day into building up my relationships? How much time do I devote to my spouse and children? How much time do I devote to God? Do I schedule a time into each day when I deliberately honor them with my full attention?* How about you? Do you prioritize full-attention family time into your week, or do they just get your end-of-the-day "time and energy leftovers"?

- How could you be more intentional in spending quality time with those who are important in your life?

- After six months of daily prayer walks, Ben had a special encounter with God where he felt His holy presence and was convicted of his sins. Have you ever had a similar encounter? Share the details of one of the times you've experienced God's presence in a special way.

Challenge: Start a prayer walk discipline, even if it's only once a week at first.

CHAPTER 5: FROM SUCCESS TO SIGNIFICANCE
- How would you define the difference between success and significance in your own words?

CHAPTER 6: THE L.I.F.E. PRINCIPLE
- Ben discovered that he had already been living out the L.I.F.E. principle in his life by sharing his Labor, Influence, Finances, and Expertise with others across the globe and in the U.S. Choose one of the four categories and share how you have helped others with that area of your L.I.F.E.

CHAPTER 7: KUBLAI KHAN ASKS FOR TEACHERS
- God miraculously opened a door for the Gospel that had been closed for 700 years, and now Ben was invited to join a mission team to Mongolia! But at first, he was too focused on his work commitments to volunteer. Going on mission teams often means we choose to spend our hard-earned vacation days and money on a ministry trip. It's quite a sacrifice. Have you ever participated on a mission trip? How did it impact your life? Was it worth the sacrifice?

CHAPTER 8: IS THIS CRAZY OR WHAT?
- Ben prayed and asked God to change his heart because he felt no love or burden for the Mongolian people at the start of his trip. He prayed for God to free him from his self-centeredness so that he could find ways to help others, and God answered his prayer. Share how helping others has helped take your mind off of your own problems and worries.

CHAPTER 9: TOM QUESTIONS THE VICE PRESIDENT

- When meeting with the Vice President, Ben and Tom learned a valuable lesson—when you are in a gathering where people are speaking a language you don't understand, you still need to be respectful and attentive. Have you ever been in a situation where people were speaking another language in front of you as if you weren't even there? How did that make you feel?

- In the age of smart phones and smart watches, it's easy to get distracted and not give your full attention when in a meeting or listening to a sermon, even in your own language. How can we discipline ourselves to be more respectful when others are speaking?

CHAPTER 10: FLY THE FRIENDLY SKIES OF MIAT

- After experiencing jetlag, unfamiliar food and smells, and a chaotic flight, Ben was ready to go home before their work had even started! Have you ever been in a similar situation of fatigue or being overwhelmed by unfamiliar customs and culture? How did you deal with that situation and what did you learn from it?

CHAPTER 11: THE LONGEST RIDE

- After a long ride across the Mongolian wilderness, followed by a disappointing fishing trip, they arrived at a place that certainly didn't meet up to their expectations of what a "resort" would look like, but the tension was diffused by having a good, long laugh together. Is there someone in your life who is always saying something witty or amusing, making you laugh even when circumstances aren't the best? How does that help you deal with stress?

CHAPTER 12: IF THIS ISN'T THE END OF THE EARTH…

- American culture focuses on being productive with our time, while many other cultures focus on building relationships and spending time together. The Mongolians valued time relaxing together playing cards, chess, or fishing, while Ben felt frustrated that he wasn't "doing something important." What can we learn from countries that have a slower pace and prioritize people over work?

CHAPTER 13: HOT TUB HEAVEN

- Ben discovered that "where you choose to focus your attention will determine your contentment level far more than the facts of the situation." Hogun chose to enjoy the hot springs without questioning where the yellow color came from, but once Ben knew the truth, he decided not to go in the hot bath and therefore didn't get relief from his back pain. Are there areas in your life where you aren't content? Could it be because you are focusing on the negative rather than being thankful for the positive? Think of three things you are thankful for in the area where you feel the most discontent.

CHAPTER 14: GOOD NEWS, BAD NEWS

- God used a desperate situation of being stranded in central Mongolia to work in Ben's heart, softening it towards the Mongolian people who live with these logistical inconveniences on a regular basis, and to give him tremendous respect for the mayor and his valuable connections which he used to solve the problem. Has God ever changed your heart towards someone after you were able to "walk in their shoes" and begin to understand their point of view?

CHAPTER 15: THE MONGOLIAN BARBECUE

- Ben and his friends won the heart of the Mongolian cook when he saw them enjoy the meal he had carefully prepared. Have you ever been in a situation where you had to struggle to eat something you disliked in order to be polite to the host or hostess? How did you manage it and what was the result?

CHAPTER 16: THIEVES, THUGS & BANDITS

- Ben was worried when he saw the thieves, thugs, and bandits waiting to steal their valuables, but the mayor used his influence to protect Ben's group and their luggage. Have you ever had something stolen? Did you feel violated by what they did or fearful that it would happen again?

- Take a moment to pray for first responders—police, firemen, and EMTs and others who sacrificially put others' safety ahead of their own.

CHAPTER 17: DON'T YOU LOVE IT WHEN A PLAN COMES TOGETHER!

- After touring Uliastai, Hogan was convinced that his American teachers could indeed live in that city. How do you think his feelings might have been different had he not first experienced the harsh conditions, shortage of transportation, and lack of modern facilities of Central Mongolia?

- In your own life, have you ever had a change of heart about a person or situation after going through a time of trials and difficulties?

CHAPTER 18: WINDOW FROM HEAVEN

- Hogan refused to leave the Mongolian interpreter behind when the pilot only wanted to take the Americans on his plane. How do you think his "no-man-left-behind" stance made the interpreter feel?

- Do you think this refusal to value Americans more than locals made a difference when he later brought over American teachers who needed guides and interpreters?

CHAPTER 19: FAREWELL TO THE MAYOR

- Why do you think the mayor who didn't believe in Christ asked Ben to pray for him before the team left?

- How might his view of Christians changed through their five days of living together in the wilderness?

CHAPTER 20: DON'T DO ANYTHING STUPID!

- Have you ever been stuck between two bad decisions and forced to choose the "lesser of two evils"? Ben chose the riskier version which would allow him to return home quicker, but they all could have died. The safer version was a 40-day trip on horseback. Are you a risk-taker or a slowly-but-surely personality?

- Which would you have chosen and why?

CHAPTER 21: THE HEART OF A TEACHER
- One of the English teachers, Doug, said that obedience was more important than safety. Do you agree? Doug was willing to risk his life to share the gospel with those living in Central Mongolia. Would you have been willing to do the same?

- Who are you willing to die for? How does that help you understand Christ's great love for us that He chose to lay down His life for us?

CHAPTER 22: A FEW PARTING THOUGHTS
- On the flight home, Ben journalled about how God had worked on their behalf, above and beyond what he had expected. Do you have a habit of keeping a journal? How does that help you stay centered and able to recognize God's leading in your life?

- If you don't keep a journal regularly, what has been the main impediment that keeps you from writing down your thoughts and prayers? Ask others for their advice.

CHAPTER 23: HOT OFF THE PRESS
- Ben didn't just move on to the next adventure after he left Mongolia—he and his wife continued to pray for the mayor and his family every night, and eventually they were able to see God answer those prayers. Are there people who you

prayed for in the past but lately have "dropped the ball" in praying for them regularly? Take a moment to jot down their names and say a quick prayer right now.

CHAPTER 24: ASSIGNMENT DEBRIEFED
- Through partnering with Hogan in ministry, as the stay-at-home part of the team, Ben and his family were able to support Hogan's ministry financially and in prayer. Hogan could safely climb the mountain only because he had a home team "securing the rope." What ministries or charities do you support? Why did you choose them?

- How have you been blessed and encouraged by hearing their ministry reports?

CHAPTER 25: WHAT ON EARTH IS "INFLUENCE"?
- Who has had a good influence on your life?

- Is there someone who has been a bad influence? What did you learn from both of these types of role models?

CHAPTER 26: THE GENERAL'S INVITATION
- Have you prayed about something and still were shocked when those prayers were answered? What were the circumstances and how did that strengthen your faith?

CHAPTER 27: TOURING THE KREMLIN
- Like the cannon that never fired and the bell that never rang, some people never discover their God-given purpose. Name some ways—big or small—where you feel you are doing what

God created you and gifted you to do. (If you have trouble recognizing what that is, think about what makes you feel the most fulfilled. It can be as simple as making soup for someone who is ill or being a greeter at church.)

CHAPTER 28: CAN I ADD THIS TO MY RESUME?

- In his radio interview, Ben chose to share about the warmth of the Russian people as his first point rather than compare the Russian lifestyle to our American freedom and abundance. Have you ever been somewhere with someone who constantly compared the food, the weather, or the cleanliness to home?

- How did that person's grumbling affect the mood of the group or hinder what you hoped to accomplish?

CHAPTER 29: STAR CITY AND COSMONAUT VOLKOV

- Russian Astronaut Yuri Gagarin was the first man in space. He loved being a cosmonaut and had trained his whole life to be in space, but the Soviet Union kept him grounded on earth because they were afraid their hero might be injured or die in an accident in space. Have you allowed fear of what others will say or fear of failure to keep you from fulfilling your dreams? What would you try to do if you were truly fearless?

CHAPTER 30: SEMINAR AT THE NUCLEAR MISSILE BASE

- What wisdom from the book of Proverbs has helped you?

- What wisdom from Proverbs do you want the next generation to embrace?

CHAPTER 31: PICKLED GARLIC CLOVES AND VODKA

- Do you know any atheists or agnostics? How does the Russian General's story give you hope for their salvation?

- How do you think General Abel's demeaner and respectful manner helped this man change his mind about God's existence?

CHAPTER 32: THE POWER OF INFLUENCE

- General Abel said, "The darker it is, the less light you need to make an impact." Have you ever been to a candlelight service where it's completely dark, but then one candle is lit, then another, and another, until the whole room is aglow? What hope does that picture give to you in your current circumstances? What hope does that give you for worldwide evangelism and its ability to bring peace to our world?

CHAPTER 33: TO BLESS OR BE BLESSED: THAT IS THE QUESTION!

- What do you feel we Americans can learn from the sacrificial hospitality shown in other nations?

- List some ways you could be more hospitable to your neighbors, co-workers, international students, or lonely people at church, and ask the Lord to guide you in whom to invite to your home, out to lunch, or to a ball game.

CHAPTER 34: MANDI AND THE SPINNING WHEELS

- It took just one week for Mandi to change her perspective of Moscow—she now remembers the people and friends she has made rather than the bleakness of the gray buildings and look of hopelessness on peoples' faces. Have you been to a country or even an inner city in our own nation where you saw the effects of poverty and hopelessness firsthand? How did that change the way you prayed for those people?

- Were you able to help in any other practical ways?

CHAPTER 35: ASSIGNMENT DEBRIEFED

- Think about the people who are in your sphere of influence right now. In what ways could you be a more proactive influencer?

- Are you able to "dream big and be creative"? If not, what about your thinking needs to change?

CHAPTER 36: A MAJOR CHALLENGE

- Have you ever made a pledge out of sheer faith or been led by the Holy Spirit to donate more than you thought you could afford? What were the results?

- How did that stretch your faith?

CHAPTER 37: A FAMILY TREASURE LOST FOR FIFTY YEARS

- Ben's aunt had been a missionary to China before the Cultural Revolution forced her to leave, but she continued to pray for the Chinese people for 50 years! Is there a part of the world where God has given you a special burden? Do you still pray regularly for those people?

- If God hasn't given you a specific place, consider praying for those who live in the 10/40 Window, where the majority of the hardest to reach Muslims, Buddhists, and Hindus live.

CHAPTER 38: ONE MISERABLE SINGAPOREAN!
- Which do you handle better, freezing cold weather or hot, humid weather?

- Share a recollection about a time when the weather affected your outlook and tried to steal your joy. Could you have prepared better?

CHAPTER 39: JET LAG & THE UPSIDE-DOWN CLOCK
- Do you suffer from jet lag when you travel? Is it worse going East or West? What has helped you adjust to the new time?

- Take time to pray for those you know who travel frequently, especially those traveling with small children and those who are physically challenged.

CHAPTER 40: ESTHER & THE MIRACLES
- Have you ever witnessed a miraculous healing or experienced it yourself? How did that testimony help strengthen your faith?

- Take a moment to pray for someone who needs healing right now.

CHAPTER 41: SEARCHING FOR LOST FAMILY TREASURE

- Like Ben, have you ever felt called by God to do something and in the midst of it felt totally discouraged and ready to give up? Share your story.

CHAPTER 42: A POWERFUL PRAYER

- Have you ever experienced a "divine appointment" or a "God-incidence"? What were the circumstances?

- Did you recognize it right away, or did it take time to realize how God had led you to that person or place?

CHAPTER 43: THE LIVER-SHAKER RIDE

- The small town in China where Ben's aunt had been a missionary had changed into a great metropolis of over a million people over the past 50 years. Have you had a similar experience of going back to a place from your youth and being shocked at the changes?

- What were your thoughts? What changes were for the better and what were for the worse?

CHAPTER 44: A DIVINE APPOINTMENT

- God had been working behind the scenes and in two hours they were led to a pastor who knew Ben's aunt! A true needle-in-the-haystack miracle! Ben said, "When you don't know what to do, do what you know." They made the first step of what they knew how to do and then God brought the right woman to help them. Have you ever been helped by a total stranger? How did they help you and how were you able to express your appreciation?

CHAPTER 45: FOUND: A LOST FAMILY TREASURE

- What do you think about the Chinese Church having no denominations?

- Do you think that could be done in our country?

- How could there be more unity in the Body of Christ?

CHAPTER 46: HOW TO BLOW AWAY AN AUNT

- Lorraine had no idea how her short time in China and continued prayers had influenced so many to become Christians. Is there someone from your childhood who helped you in your spiritual journey?

- What would you like to tell them when you see them again in heaven?

CHAPTER 47: THE RAG-TAG TEAM

- Have you ever had a nudge from the Holy Spirit to pray for someone seemingly out of the blue? What were the circumstances?

- Have you ever had someone contact you, saying they felt led to pray for you and wanted to make sure you were alright? How did you feel when you learned they were praying for you? We may never know on earth how these prayers have protected us and our loved ones!

CHAPTER 48: A WHITE-HAIRED GRANDMA GOES TO HONG KONG

- Mission teams aren't just for the young and active! What are the challenges people face traveling in their senior years?

- How would having middle-aged or senior volunteers on a mission team be beneficial and help the ministry?

CHAPTER 49: JAMES CHU: THE HAMBURGER MAN

- Have you ever felt exhausted, then began to help someone else and felt suddenly rejuvenated? What were the circumstances?

- Have you gone to visit someone who was sick or grieving with the intention of encouraging them but ended up being encouraged yourself? Share an example of "being blessed to be a blessing."

CHAPTER 50: CRAMMING SEVEN DAYS INTO SEVEN HOURS

- Do you think modern transportation keeps us from experiencing the beauty of nature and real life of the local people that we would have discovered on the slower means of travel in the past? What are the pros and cons?

- Share a story of when you either enjoyed or were forced to endure "slow transportation."

CHAPTER 51: THE GREAT REUNION

- Have you ever been reunited with someone you haven't seen in years, and it seemed like you were able to pick right up where you left off as if no time had passed? Share about your reunion.

CHAPTER 52: THE DAM PROJECT & THE WANZHOU CHURCH SPLIT

- Although the Chinese church split was due to logistics and not a rift in the congregation, dividing a church into two new congregations must have been heart-breaking. Share your experience with a church split and why it happened. Were they able to continue to flourish as separate congregations or did they "lose sheep" in the process?

CHAPTER 53: HOW IT FEELS TO BE A ROCK STAR

- Jake realized that God had given him influence with the Chinese teens just by being an American with light hair. It was nothing he had earned or studied for—he was just born that way. In what ways has God given you the ability to help others just because of things such as your family background, being raised in the church or on a farm, or perhaps growing up in a bilingual or mixed-culture neighborhood?

CHAPTER 54: 101 WAYS TO WOK YOUR DOG

- What is the most unusual food you have ever eaten? Did you like it? Is there an exotic food you'd like to try?

- What part of the world would be the most challenging for you to eat their food every day?

CHAPTER 55: DEVIL CITY

- In the past, many people received Christ because they were afraid to go to hell, but nowadays, churches don't talk much about the devil or hell. Why do you think that is?

- Do you agree or disagree with the modern church trends to be "seeker sensitive"?

CHAPTER 56: GRANDMA GETS HER GIFT

- From that ministry trip, Cora received the blessing of a Chinese spiritual son, daughter-in-law, and grandchildren. Do you have any spiritual children or spiritual parents (people who share your faith and are like family to you)? How did God bring you together?

CHAPTER 57: ASSIGNMENT DEBRIEFED

- Have you developed the spiritual discipline of giving the Lord a tenth of your income? From time to time, has God led you to go above and beyond the tithe to meet special needs? How has He done that?

- Might He be calling you again to help with a special need? Are you prepared to say "yes" when He does? Ask the Lord to show you other needs you can help meet as He blesses you and gives you the ability to bless others.

CHAPTER 58: FORREST GUMP OR INDIANA JONES?

- Although we may dream of having exciting "Indiana Jones"-like adventures, for most of us, we will be more like Forrest Gump—God will use us where we are right now to meet the ordinary needs of ordinary people. Can you give an example of God using you because you were in the right place at the right time? It can be as simple as giving money to a homeless person on a street corner or helping an older person carry their groceries—a small thing to you but a big thing to the recipient.

CHAPTER 59: SURE, I'D LIKE TO VISIT JUAN VALDEZ

- Rather than deciding to go on the trip based on his own rosy-tinted-glasses-view, Ben reached out to his friend, General Abel, to get a more accurate view of the situation they would face in Colombia. Who do you go to when you need honest advice, even if they disagree with you?

- Why do you value their opinion?

CHAPTER 60: A STRANGE & FUNNY MEETING

- Ben considered every missions journey as a team effort—while he went on a ministry trip, his wife stayed home with the kids and prayed. Nancy was brave enough to trust the Lord if it was His will for Ben to go to Colombia, even though the research she'd done on the internet talked about the many dangers. Do you think you would have trusted God like Nancy? Why or why not?

- Often, we try to hide the truth about danger or illness from our loved ones, but that only keeps them from praying with the whole truth at a time when honest prayers are needed more than ever! How about you? Do you try to shelter your friends and relatives from knowing the truth when it's negative because you don't want them to worry? What does that say about your belief in the power of prayer?

CHAPTER 61: RUNNING THE GAUNTLET AT THE COLOMBIAN AIRPORT

- Although he was afraid for his life, none of Ben's fears came true as he arrived in Colombia. Psalm 91:1 (911) helped calm his spirit when he was afraid. What helps you when you're feeling afraid or caught up in worries and anxiety? Do you call out to God with 911?

CHAPTER 62: DRUG HIT MAN A.K.A. OUR BODY GUARD

- Like a modern-day Saul of Tarsus, the team's driver had formally worked for the drug cartel and was now working to protect Christians. Sometimes it's easy to "write someone off" and not even try to share the Gospel with someone we see as being on the enemy's side. Do you think you would have witnessed to a man like their driver?

- Would you have believed him when he said he had switched to God's side?

CHAPTER 63: A PLAN UNFOLDS

- When hearing about the plan to reach businessmen in Colombia, Ben immediately thought they should invite someone famous to speak to the people, but God's plan was to use Ben himself! Often, it's easy for us to point to someone whom we feel is more qualified rather than to just say, "Here am I, send me" (Is. 6:8). Have you ever been able to help someone or be used in ministry even though you weren't the most qualified? Share about your experience.

CHAPTER 64: LEAVING OUR HEARTS IN COLOMBIA

- Although originally afraid to even visit Colombia, Ben grew to love it and found it hard to leave. Has God ever changed your heart about a place where you first had no desire to visit or live there? What happened and how long did it take?

CHAPTER 65: JOURNAL NOTES & QUOTES

- Ben's son, Jacob, said to his mom: "There's no place safer than in the center of God's will." Like with Shadrach, Meshach, and Abednego in the fiery furnace, God didn't remove the danger for Ben's team in Colombia. Instead, He provided peace and divine protection in the midst of the danger. God gave them an experienced and knowledgeable driver who knew how to avoid the ways in which foreign businessmen were often kidnapped. When have you prayed for God to remove a problem, but instead experienced peace and divine protection in the midst of that situation?

CHAPTER 66: YOU WANT ME TO SPEAK IN COLOMBIA?

- Because of mistakes he'd made in business, Ben felt disqualified to share his "expertise" with the Colombian businessmen. How has God used a failure in your life to help or give advice to someone else?

CHAPTER 67: TOTAL SUCCESS 4X2

- Many Colombians wouldn't step foot in a church but would go to a conference to hear Christian businessmen share their testimonies. Does your church have an outreach to reach those in your community who normally don't go to church (perhaps a food distribution program or seasonal events)? Share what they do and how effective you believe it is.

- If not, how might you help the church to start an outreach or join forces with parachurch ministries such as Samaritan's Purse Christmas Child, Angel Tree Prison Fellowship, or your local rescue mission?

CHAPTER 68: MY COMPETITIVE ADVANTAGE: FOUR KEYS TO SUCCESS

- Which one of Ben's four disciplines (Read, Walk, Work, and Listen) is the most challenging for you to fit into your daily schedule?

CHAPTER 69: A HEART IS CHANGED

- The first people to whom Ben was able to minister weren't the businessmen he thought he'd reach, but two children of a large furniture factory owner. Ben still took the time to share his message with those two children. What can we learn from this example?

CHAPTER 70: THE QUALITIES OF LEADERSHIP THAT MONEY CAN'T BUY

- Tom describes teamwork as: "People contributing their own strong points while covering the other member's weak points." He explains that it's important to understand your teammate's weakness and then purposefully cover it with your strength. How have you seen that principle operate in your workplace? In your marriage and family?

CHAPTER 71: PEP RALLY 101

- Proverbs 29:18 says: "Without a vision, the people perish." Do you regularly set goals for both your personal and business life? Why or why not?

- What is your vision for the next year? The next five years? Ten years?

- Have you shared that vision with your family so they can help you meet your goals as a team, or do you act like a "lone wolf" trying to accomplish everything on your own?

CHAPTER 72: ASSIGNMENT DEBRIEFED

Answer Ben's two questions posed in this chapter:

- Is God prompting you to use your expertise in a way that stretches you beyond your comfort zone?

- Do you have something to share with others that you never really thought about before?

CHAPTER 73: HOW TO DEVELOP YOUR ETERNAL BUSINESS PLAN

- How might you use your L.I.F.E. for eternal purposes? Jot down some ideas and ask God for confirmation.

CHAPTER 74: PROS & CONS OF OVERSEAS MISSIONS

- Though expensive and time-consuming, family mission trips helped Ben and Nancy's children to be more thankful for their blessings and to be less selfish. How might you encourage others in your life to discover their giftings and blessings?

- Part of Nancy's labor and expertise is used on the Homefront through her gifts of hospitality and intercessory prayer. How have you been used on the Homefront in support of ministries or missions?

CHAPTER 75: WHAT CAN YOU EXPECT?

- Ben said that God did not open new doors for them until they began to do those things that He had already made clear in Scripture. Is there an area of your life where you have not yet obeyed Christ's directive?

- What first steps can you take to be obedient?

CHAPTER 76: TIME MANAGEMENT 101

- What is God showing you through the story of the rocks and the jar? What are the big rocks in your life?

- What smaller stones should you remove from your jar to make room for what God has shown you to prioritize?

CHAPTER 77: WHY DO YOU GIVE?
- Do you sometimes give out of guilt, duty, or generosity? Ben shared his reasons for giving are: training, obedience, personal relationships, purpose, and his love for Jesus. Which of these areas would you like to grow in as you give?

CHAPTER 78: WHY DO YOU DO WHAT YOU DO?
Try to write out your worldview in only a few sentences. You may want to read Appendix D first to give you ideas.

CHAPTER 79: THE GREAT DISCONNECT
- Do you hold one of the three major worldviews or a mixture of two or three?
- Is God prompting you to re-evaluate your worldview or become more consistent?

CHAPTER 80: FINISHING STRONG
At the end of this chapter, Ben challenged us with these two questions:

- What are you doing today that will last beyond your lifetime?
- What goals might you strive toward that you enable you to finish strong?

CHAPTER 81: THE BOOK OF L.I.F.E.

- Do you have a vacation planned in the near future? Where do you plan to go and with whom?

- Could you add a prayer walk or a visit to local churches to your itinerary? You will find your vacation much more meaningful with eternal value if you do! If possible, find out the needs of the churches you visit and pray about how to help them.

APPENDICES

APPENDIX A:
The Lord's Prayer

RELATIONSHIP (REVELATION 4-5)
Our Father, Who art in heaven…
- Reaffirm your relationship with God.
- Express thankfulness that you are a child of God by adoption into His family.

PRAISE
Hallowed be Thy name…
- Praise will lead into worship, so speak out words of praise.
- Ponder God's greatness, majesty, awesomeness. Thank Him for His divine attributes, such as "Thank You for Your goodness and mercy, thank You for Your Healing power," etc.
- Pray Psalms 8, 23, 29, 33, 93, 96, 103, 111, 139, 145. Try summarizing these verses and put them in your own words or use this time to recite verses you have memorized.

PERSPECTIVE

Thy kingdom come, Thy will be done on earth as it is in heaven…
- Pray for His will to be done in your life and family.
- Intercede for the world—countries suffering from wars or natural disasters and nations that forbid the Gospel to be preached.
- Pray for missions. Pray specifically for missionaries by name or missionary organizations and intercede for their needs.
- Pray for government and political leaders.
- Pray for social and criminal injustice to be revealed and reversed.
- Pray for the triumph of the Church over the schemes of the enemy.
- Express your longing for Christ's return.

PROVISION

Give us this day our daily bread…
- Express thanks for:
    a) Food, clothing, and shelter.
    b) Meaningful work.
    c) Ability to serve.
    d) Ability to give.

FORGIVENESS (PSALM 5)

And forgive us our trespasses, as we forgive those who trespass against us…
- Confess specific sins and attitudes.
- Ask for forgiveness.

- Forgive others who have wronged you this week.

PROTECTION (JAMES 1:12-16, 1 COR. 10:13)

And lead us not into temptation, but deliver us from evil.

- Acknowledge your proneness to fall into sin.
- Tell God about the trials and testing you are facing.
- Thank God for trials that build character into our lives.

OWNERSHIP (PSALM 72:19, MATTHEW 6:33)

*For **Thine** is the kingdom and the power and the glory, forever and ever.*

- Acknowledge that God is the Owner, and we are just the stewards of everything on this earth.
- Pray over the things that God has entrusted you with on this earth, that they will be in accordance with His eternal plans. Speak aloud in worship, saying statements such as: "God, everything I have is yours. It's not my business—it's Yours. Jesus, You are the CEO. I am Your legs and arms to accomplish the work You have given me, but all the results are up to You. You are the owner of my home and all my possessions. Thank You for letting me use these things that are ultimately Yours. Thank You for the privilege of raising my family. You have entrusted this family to me, but my kids and grandkids are Yours, not mine."

APPENDIX B:
Four Daily Disciplines that Lead to Personal Success

1. **Read a chapter of Proverbs each morning.**

   Each morning, spend fifteen minutes with the wisest man who ever lived—King Solomon. The book of Proverbs has 31 chapters, so read the chapter that corresponds to that day of the month to receive wisdom for the day.

2. **Take a "Prayer Walk," praying through the Lord's Prayer** and apply each section to the events of your day. Spend time working on relationships with God, your spouse and children, coworkers and clients—everyone in your sphere of influence.

   In the morning before you go to work, take a walk and pray through the Lord's Prayer, applying each section to the events of your day. Each of us has a potential positive or negative impact on others and in order to keep our influence positive, we need to get our attitude straight for the day. If you prefer to walk in the evening, pray through the Lord's Prayer and apply each section to your next day's schedule. You can also take that time to thank the Lord for how He has answered your prayers and guided you through the day that is coming to an end.

3. **Work based on your worldview and core values**—think about how you can work with integrity, honoring your commitments with quality work. Focus your energy to provide financially for your family and also help to fulfill the Great Commission.

    For example, recently, my company was awarded the largest job in the history of our business. We were not the lowest bidder, nor were we the most qualified to do the work, but we won the job because we had a reputation for honesty and integrity.

4. **Listen with an open heart to hear what God is trying to teach you. Be willing to change as a result of what God shows you.**

    At the end of each day, take time to relax and evaluate your day with an open heart to hear what God is trying to teach you. It's easy to rush through life so fast that you can miss this important step of reflection, and the lessons you learn will merely stay in your head without reaching into your heart and life. It takes time to process new concepts. Ask yourself, "How will this lesson affect my life? What do I need to change as a result of what I learned today?" Then take time to listen for God's answer. Doing this will develop real meaning and direction in your life.

APPENDIX C:
Favorite Quotes

We will have all eternity to celebrate our victories, but only a few short hours before sunset in which to win them.
—ROBERT MOFFAT

God's plan done in God's way and God's timing will never lack God's provision.
—HUDSON TAYLOR

I.G.T. = "In God's Timing"
—DICK ABEL

Calamity clarifies. Comfort confuses. Persecution purifies. Prosperity can pollute.
—KEVIN TURNER

Prosperity = having everything you need to accomplish the will of God in your life.
—AUTHOR UNKNOWN

Be a thermostat which impacts your environment.
Not a thermometer which reflects your environment.
—RON HUTCHCRAFT

The challenge of the super intellect is to
make complex things simple.
—HENRY DAVID THOREAU

The end does not justify the means.
—THE BIBLE, JOHN 6

You can do some things I cannot do.
I can do some things you cannot do.
Together we can do some great things.
—MOTHER TERESA

God does not want us to do something great for Him. Rather,
He wants us to be obedient and watch Him do something great.
—DAVID BEHLING

In America, you have big church but small God.
In third world, we have small church but big God.
—MEXICAN PASTOR

Work as if prayer meant nothing.
Pray as if work meant nothing.
That's the proper balance.
—MARTIN LUTHER

Everyone wants to have a testimony,
but to have a testimony, you must have a victory.
To have a victory, you must be involved in the battle.
But the battle can be a dangerous and difficult place.
—KEVIN TURNER

My prayer is that when the Lord returns, He will find me
involved in the battle and not on the sidelines watching.
—DAVE HANNAH

If not you, then who? If not now, then when?
—JOHN F. KENNEDY

APPENDIX D:
Register Here for Special Agent Opportunities

The options for investing your L.I.F.E. in His Majesty's Service are unlimited!

Besides investing our hearts and resources into the ministries of our local churches, our extended family has partnered with the following list of ministries that empowered us to experience what God is doing around the world. We are pleased to recommend them to you.

- **The local church**: Get involved in your own community and circle of influence.
- **Big Life**: Get trained to make disciples of Jesus in your corner of the world at https://big.life
- **The Church Doctor**: help your church evaluate its strengths/weaknesses and motivate members into action. See www.churchdoctorministries.com
- **Answers in Genesis**: Discover resources to help build a solid foundation for the Christian faith. See www.answersingenesis.org

- **World Concern**: Provide loans for third-world microenterprises at www.worldconcern.org
- **Orphan Helpers**: Help transform the lives of abandoned, abused, and incarcerated youth across El Salvador, Honduras and Guatemala at www.orphanhelpers.org
- **CRU**: Explore training, discipleship, and outreach resources to fulfill the Great Commission in our generation. (We partnered with the Military Ministry, which provides spiritual resources for families through Marriage and Family Ministries.) Check out their different ministries at www.cru.org
- **YWAM**: Youth With A Mission focuses on "Knowing God and Making Him Known." Attend a five-month training/outreach school called Crossroads (for those over 30), after which you can get involved in any area of expertise (i.e., Join a medical team on a mercy ship) at www.ywam.org
- **ELIC**: Enjoy opportunities to teach English abroad at www.elic.org
- **Christian Jobs**: Match your "special agent" expertise with opportunities in many different organizations for full-time service at www.christianjobs.com.

www.ingramcontent.com/pod-product-compliance
Lightning Source LLC
Chambersburg PA
CBHW060550080526
44585CB00013B/509